Also by Linda Eyre (with Richard Eyre)

Teaching Your Children Sensitivity
Three Steps to a Strong Family
Teaching Your Children Values
Teaching Your Children Responsibility
Teaching Your Children Joy

I Didn't Plan to Be a Witch

◆

and Other Surprises of a Joyful Mother

◆

Linda Eyre

A Fireside Book
Published by Simon & Schuster
NEW YORK LONDON TORONTO SYDNEY TOKYO SINGAPORE

FIRESIDE
Rockefeller Center
1230 Avenue of the Americas
New York, NY 10020

FIRESIDE and colophon are registered trademarks
of Simon & Schuster Inc.

Designed by Elina D. Nudelman
Illustrations by Terry Ravanelli

Manufactured in the United States of America

1   3   5   7   9   10   8   6   4   2

Library of Congress Cataloging-in-Publication Data
Eyre, Linda.
I didn't plan to be a witch : and other surprises of a joyful
mother / Linda Eyre.
p. cm.
Originally published: Salt Lake City : Publishers Press, 1988.
"A Fireside book."
1. Mothers—United States—Biography. 2. Motherhood—United
States—Case studies. 3. Mother and child—United States—Case
studies. 4. Family—United States—Case studies. 5. Parenting—
United States.   I. Title
HQ759.E95   1996
306.874'3—dc20   95-51560
                                                          CIP

ISBN 0-684-80785-8

✦ contents ✦

✦ preface ✦

I love surprises, which, I guess, is why I love being a mother. Motherhood is just one big surprise after another. Some are not really pleasant surprises. One of my first ones was that I could become, at almost a moment's notice, a magnificent witch. Yet there is something about the bonding experience of motherhood that makes the rewards and joys far outweigh the struggles and trials. Just as I think I am sacrificing for my children, I realize that I am really the one who is benefitting from the sacrifice.

There has probably never been a generation of mothers under more stress. Not only are our lives filled with the stress of everyday living, but we see other mothers who look so well adjusted and organized, with happy, smiling children, which just sends us off on a stress/guilt trip. Our own lives seem so chaotic and our kids do such strange things. We wonder what we are doing wrong.

I am here with this book to offer a surprise: The longer I live, the more I am convinced that there are moms that are super, but there are really no supermoms. No one really feels that they are having it all and doing it all, all at once. Every mother struggles with dastardly doubts, challenging children, crazy crises, and wicked witchhood. Every mother experiences the heights and the depths of human experience through motherhood. Yet there has also never been a generation of better, more dedicated mothers. I see mothers in every possible situation, usually under mountains of stress, who are going to extraordinary lengths to be incredible mothers. Good mothers are the backbone of any great nation. But mothering is a lonely job. Even though we have common experiences, our circumstances are so unique. We have all been married to different people and our children all have unique needs. It is therefore ever more important that we strengthen the spine with commendation, commiseration, and communication!

When people ask me if I really *planned* to have nine children, I solemnly shake my head and say, "No, I planned to have ten." I am a glutton for surprises! Every child has blessed my life immensely, and though I started out thinking I would like to make them better people, as it has turned out, each has made *me* better. In fact, there are moments when they are students, but they have mostly become my teachers. For this I am truly a "joyful mother of children." (Psalms 113:9)

Our children's ages today are Saren twenty-five, Shawni twenty-three, Josh twenty-one, Saydi nineteen, Jonah eighteen, Talmadge sixteen, Noah fourteen, Eli twelve, and Charity nine. Since I have been trying to write this book over the span of twenty-five years, you will find them at different ages in different chapters. All stories have been printed with their permission. You may be interested to see, as I have been, how consistent their personalities are, even though they are described at different ages. Luckily, we have been blessed with one of every kind. Not just five sons and four daughters, but nine children who possess every personality trait imaginable. I say luckily because it makes for a better book—you can just about be certain that you will see your own child in one of ours—complete with angels' halos and devils' horns.

After the Prologue and first "Surprise," this book is not designed to be read in any particular order, as it was not written in order. Read it according to what appeals to you or what you feel you need to hear most. I hope it provides you some assistance and a few concrete ideas, but most of all I trust that it will provide a little comic relief when you've had a bad day. Somehow, it gives mothers such solace to know that they're not the only ones who have days when they feel they are living in a Roadrunner cartoon that just won't end.

I have tried to capture some of the hilarious, mind-boggling intricacies of mothering that we have all experienced in an attempt to help the "sisterhood" of mothers feel more comforted in their witchhood, more normal amidst uncanny disasters, more joyful in their careers as mothers, and more excited about their own surprises.

✦ credits ✦

To open with, you should know that when equally strong-willed Richard and I were married, we really believed that we were soulmates . . . two souls who were meant to be together from before time began. Twenty-six years, ten thousand arguments, and nine children later, we believe even more surely that we are soulmates. Not only that, we prayed fervently with each pregnancy that the Lord would send us good and valiant souls, and pledged that we would do our best to guide them to fulfill their destiny.

With every passing year, we see the answers to our prayers beyond our wildest dreams—along with the understanding that our trials are our greatest teachers. Because of all that, not only our daily lives but our spiritual lives hold us together.

The credit for this book really goes to my dear mother, who, since the completion of this book, has passed on to a much higher realm at age ninety. Enormous credit also goes to Richard, an ever supportive husband and incredible father who is also lots of fun (and lots of trouble) and just a little bit crazy, and to our nine superb children, who I love more than my life, and who gave consent to this mother to have the gory details of their lives in print so that other mothers might feel more normal; and to a loving Heavenly Father to whom we owe it all.

Credit also goes to those struggling mothers who love their children as much as I do mine, but who are not as lucky as I have been: homeless mothers, abused mothers, unwed mothers, and single mothers. To them I dedicate this book, not only in thought but in deed, as I commit to set aside money received from royalties from this book to help fortify them. Mothers are the backbone of any society. Maybe we can strengthen that spine just a bit . . . one mother at a time.

✦ prologue: ✦
the journey of motherhood

For months I had put writing this book once more on the back burner. Life was so complicated. Spring was filled with moving home after a nine-month stay in Washington, D.C. Two weeks later, I was bestowed the unexpected full-time job of caring for a bed-bound son whose life was miraculously spared after being hit by a car. Summer brought traveling to Eastern Europe to retrieve two daughters who had just finished eighteen months of humanitarian service and missionary work in Bulgaria and Romania, and preparing the festivities of a joyful homecoming for them. The day after that, I was worried about getting haircuts and wardrobe for ten of us who were going to do a television show that week in New York with Kathy Lee and Frank Gifford. In the meantime, hundreds of hours were being spent on a major overhaul of our sadly neglected house, including wringing my hands over a remodeling project. This involved surviving myriads of arguments with a strong-willed husband about what the windows should be like, what color to paint the walls, and what size the bookshelves should be. I was much too busy mothering and wifing to write about it.

Finally, after another four months of seemingly impossible hurdles and a particularly nasty outbreak of "witchhood," I decided the time had come to finish this book. Since it is impossible for me to sit in my own house and not be distracted by things like a kitchen floor that looks as though Hansel and Gretel have recently been through leaving their trail of crumbs, a water softener needing salt, light bulbs all over the house needing to be replaced, and a laundry hamper like a volcano about to erupt, I announced that I was leaving—by myself, for five days, to go through my efforts of the last several years and begin to organize them into a book.

Although I had done this many times in the past for twenty-four-hour periods, you must understand that living with eleven hungry stomachs, twenty-two knees wearing holes through jeans, eleven pairs of feet always in need of new shoes (or sometimes *any* shoes), and one-hundred-ten fingers spilling milk, leaving drawers open, and opening fridge doors made it almost impossible to desert for very long!

I do have a terrific husband, whose schedule can be abnormally flexible, and to whom I turned over the entire responsibility of the household, at his suggestion. I smiled as I drove away, knowing that Richard's strength is really in handling the "big picture." By that I mean he loves to do the really meaningful things with the kids, like telling them stories about their ancestors and turning into a character called "Monster Man" or "Tinkerbell" at bedtime who teaches them a valuable lesson for life. The children are totally immersed in a fantasy world and have such great fun. *But,* when it comes to menial details, that is a different story. "He'll never notice the kitchen crumbs," I thought. "And when Noah wails that he doesn't have a clean jersey for his basketball game, Richard will just tell him to wear it straight out of the hamper, reasoning that it will smell bad by the end of the first quarter of the game anyway." I did pass through a moment of horror when I realized that there was a small chance he might actually *do* the laundry. I hate pink underwear!

Having stocked the house with food and left some semblance of order, I began my journey with a sense of great anticipation. I spent my first day away on a six-hour drive from our home through several mountain passes in the dead of winter to Jackson Hole, Wyoming. So much can happen in a mind in six uninterrupted hours with the only distraction the scenery passing by.

The night before, I had stayed up until 1:30 A.M. helping our high school senior with "the most important paper of the year—on Symbolism." I couldn't help seeing the symbolism of my journey as the hours passed. How like the process of mothering was that day as I experienced new adventures and multiple surprises.

Within the first hour, I was near the top of one of the highest mountains in the Wasatch Range. My first surprise was a blizzard: The wind was blowing and I could barely see the road. "This was a dumb thing to try without watching the weather forecast," I thought. "I didn't realize it would be this hard, but I can't turn back now. I'm going to have to go slow and just do the best I can. Maybe I should stop and let this thing blow over." Other drivers suddenly became irritating to me as they followed too closely or moved so slowly that I thought we were all going to come to a standstill and never get the momentum to make it to the top of the mountain pass. Several cars whose drivers had obviously made some serious mistakes were plowed nose-first into a snowdrift. One was tipped sideways and plowed into a huge mound of snow. I was scared and had to remind myself to gear down, drive defensively, and not touch the brakes. Just as I was about to give up, I encountered another surprise: The snow stopped and the road ahead improved.

The next two hours were tedious. I traveled over dry roads, then snow-packed roads, then through another snowstorm. Each stretch of road seemed to hold a new challenge. Time dragged and I began to wonder if I would ever get there. Just when I thought I was in for snow and treacherous going the rest of the way, totally dry roads and a sparkling evening sky appeared.

After dark, I felt saturated from hearing the same news on the radio for the twentieth time, and called home on my cellular phone to ask our eight-year-old how to turn on the new CD deck in Dad's car, which I was driving. She obliged with some impatience at my stupidity. The music transformed my thinking. Somehow the quiet, thoughtful music on each of the five CDs that Richard had left in his deck seemed meant for me. It lifted me to a different paradigm. Something about it changed my mind-set and an almost ethereal experience began. Suddenly I was no longer worried about "getting there" and had started truly "enjoying the journey." The winter wonderland that stretched before me as far as my headlights could reach was a feast for the eyes. Snowflakes, sometimes gently sifting, sometimes wildly flying through the air, and the sparkle of clear air on wide, pine-tree-lined roads, transformed the trials of the journey into a great adventure. In one mountain pass, a huge young moose, startled by my headlights, moved to the other side of the white-carpeted road and watched me slowly roll by. Everything my eyes rested on was beautiful, and I began to wish that the journey would never end.

As in motherhood, the storms, the feelings of self-doubt, irritation, worry, fear, and second-guessing were all there, along with moments of joy in knowing that, hard as it is, there is no place else I'd rather be. The frustration of trying to "get there" and the peace of slowing down and "enjoying the journey" are at the core of my experience as a mother.

It also occurred to me that the warm glow of light from each scattered little farmhouse along the way, almost obscured by snow in a Currier and Ives setting, represented a family. As I listened to "On a Bleak Midwinter Evening" on the CD, I realized that each house probably contained a mother who was experiencing the same joys and frustrations that have been experienced by mothers throughout time.

Ironically, toward the end of my journey, I drove through Star Valley, Wyoming, where my eighty-nine-year-old mother had been born and raised in a little farmhouse, one of a family of ten children. Stories flashed back into my mind that she had told so many times. During the school year, she and three of her teen-aged siblings attended high school in the nearest "big town." Stocked with a ten-gallon can of milk and homemade bread for their only sustenance, they hopped into a horse-drawn sleigh in midwinter for the thirty-mile journey. They would usually return home for the weekend on Friday after dark, with temperatures that she remembers as between 40 and 50 below zero. (Teenagers never did have any sense.)

I thought of those kids, about the same ages as our present teenagers, bundled up in mounds of homemade quilts and rough-hewn blankets . . . feet cuddled up and fighting for space on the hot bricks heated thoroughly on the old pot-bellied stove just before they left. Uncle Wilford, the oldest brother, was the driver, urging the horses on their three- to four-hour journey home through the same kind of sparkling, crackling snow that I was whizzing past. I smiled over how much times have changed as I glided the same distance in less than thirty minutes, warm and snug in my car, with my cellular phone, listening to superb music on a CD. Yet I'm sure their mother experienced the same age-old emotions of worry about those teenagers getting home safely as I do about ours driving home safely on a snowy Friday night.

My grandmother died in the flu epidemic of 1918 (along with her two youngest babies), so I never got a chance to ask her about her experience as a mother. But surely she had her share of mothering "blizzards," wanting to turn back, struggling with the journey without giving up. There must have been days when she was overcome by irritation and anger, and days when she was surprised about who she was because of what her children taught her. Certainly she experienced her share of the joy of seeing a child actually internalize a principle she had taught them as she began to watch them become interesting, contributing members of society.

I am sure that there were moments when she wanted to just quit, and days and maybe even sometimes whole pregnancies when she hardly recognized herself. Just as we do, she probably committed to be the best mother in the world before the arrival of each child—kind, loving, patient; always there with hot cookies, a listening ear, and a positive attitude. Then to her surprise she undoubtedly discovered that the stress and strain of daily demands often made that seem crazy. She probably also discovered that common, ordinary children have an incredible knack of driving an otherwise normal, fun-loving mother to the brink of insanity. She must have found, just as we do, that there are moments when we put on our witch hat, stick a wart on our noses, and screech things like, "Don't bother me!" "I can't talk about that right now!" and, "That was a *stupid* thing to do!"

Just as surely as there were trying moments, there were also moments when those same children swept her to a higher realm, where the mundane seemed momentous and drudgery turned to delight. So it was recently with me when our eight-year-old handed me a homemade gift at the end of a particularly grueling day. Her gift consisted of an eight- by eight-inch board which she insisted I must place on my bedroom dresser where I could see it every morning as I "hit the day."

On it she had pasted a happy face and this message in her own happy scrawl: "Have Joy and Hope Before you go. Love Charity."

Even though motherhood is a universal experience, there are as many different mothers and circumstances as there are families. While you may be "snowed" thinking about the ramifications of raising nine children, I am absolutely in awe of mothers who are single, working and struggling to be both mother and father; amazed at older mothers who are beginning their mothering careers at forty (as my mother did); and overwhelmed thinking of the challenges of dealing with an only child, adopted children, foster children, stepchildren, rebellious children, abused children, gifted children, or disabled children.

Still, as I have observed mothers all over the world—from Japan to Bulgaria and from Sri Lanka to Mexico—I have realized that motherhood is the great equalizer. No matter what the economic level, the living conditions, or other extraneous circumstances that exist in our lives, we all want the same thing: To help our children reach the greatness within them and to survive the process ourselves. In the course, a magical thing happens: We actually become better for the wear.

Yes, motherhood is a trip. Besides being rigorous and rewarding, it is also fun and often hysterical. So, as we journey through this very real, warts-and-all book together and experience the lower and higher realms of motherhood, including witchhood and myriads of surprises, I can almost feel your arm around my shoulder and mine around yours as we laugh and cry, wring hands, sometimes feel guilty, but above all enjoy together that most joyous and important of life's experiences . . . motherhood.

Linda Eyre
Jackson Hole, Wyoming
January 1995

Surprise One
I Didn't Plan to Be a Witch!

I always thought that I was going to be the perfect mom. After all, I had seen perfect moms on TV and in the movies all my life. Visions danced in my head of happy, giggling children . . . little girls with curly hair tied up with flamboyant bows that just matched their dresses, which I had made for them with my own hands, and clean, well-mannered little boys with knickers, suspenders, and bow ties and freckled-faced impish grins. Images of mothers who were in control and sympathetic, and had a warm smile and a sensible solution for every problem, made mothering seem fun and exciting. I could hardly wait to be the beaming mother in the audience, watching MY children perform.

Knowing that I wanted a large family, and armed with my two favorite quotes on the fridge—"No success can compensate for failure in the home," from David O. McKay, and, "The greatest work you will ever do will be within the walls of your own home," from Harold B. Lee—I launched into my mothering career.

I remembered sensing the need for some adjustments in my thinking one day as I tried to cut out a dress pattern for our three-year-old as she busily dumped out the straight pins and cut up the other pattern pieces with the scissors. After a few years, I gave up sewing altogether, except in cases of absolute emergency.

Those little boys' impish grins actually turned out to be mischievous ones. My visions of fun did not include a neighbor calling me and saying, "Drop the phone! Your little boys are out on the roof!" Keeping them clean, let alone bow-tied, was about as likely as Mother Teresa marrying Saddam Hussein.

Years went by, and I actually got used to the surprise that I was not the perfect mother I had envisioned. In fact, there were lots of moments when I resembled the Wicked Witch who dropped in and crashed the party at Sleeping Beauty's house. I'm not talking about the abuse kind of witchhood, but the kind of witchhood that arrives after a hard day full of pressures and worries and frustrations when some child or husband says something that is the one "last straw" that drives you over the edge. I keep thinking that I will get over these witch attacks, but even though I must admit that they are happening less often, I'm still susceptible. Look in with me at a day last week that led up to my most recent attack.

It was one of those days when I could have used a sweatshirt with a red-blinking, battery-operated "ON OVERLOAD" sign on the front. That would have helped everybody concerned. The past few days had been grueling. We had made *ten* TV shows in Dallas the day before. After finishing the last one, Richard headed for New York and I dashed to the airport to see if I could get home soon enough to hear the last half of our senior, Jonah's, final a capella concert at the high school. He hadn't thought to mention that it was happening until we were on our way out the door. Still, it was the last a capella performance in his high school career and I was determined that I, the mother who prided herself on being at every kid's performance, could get there before the final curtain fell.

After being preoccupied all day with whether or not I could make it, I was relieved when the plane left on time. I knew that I was going to make it, confident that I could still catch the last half hour, until we landed and then sat on the runway for some mysterious reason for half an hour while I despised the airline and wrung my hands. In a panic, I dashed past the baggage claim on a dead run, thinking I'd come back later for my bag. When I got to the high school, after having broken the speed limit and screeched around the final corner to the school, the last five kids in choir uniform were just leaving the auditorium. A combination of guilt, nostalgia, stress, and exhaustion enveloped me like a blanket and I cried like a baby all the way back to the airport to get my bag. And all the way home. By the time Jonah saw me, I was a basket case. My eyes were red and puffy, and my face felt like a balloon about to pop. "I'm so sorry," I blubbered. "I tried so hard!"

"Mom," Jonah quickly assured me, "don't worry. It's not that bad! The kids were there. Don't cry. It scares me. You never cry. Really, I know I'm still your first priority. Everything's okay!" Jonah's a great kid. I was supposed to make him feel better, and instead he had comforted me.

The next day was also full of demands. My anxiety level peaked that afternoon. By 5:00 P.M., I needed to shop for and prepare a birthday dinner for Jonah. By 6:00, I had to leave to give a speech. This was Jonah's momentous birthday: number eighteen. In retrospect, I don't know why this birthday seemed *so* important. He didn't plan to start drinking, and I wasn't worried about the draft, but eighteen just sounded so significant. It was probably more crucial to me than it was to him, in light of having just missed his concert the night before, worrying about his upcoming graduation and the inevitable leaving home for college in just a few months.

In addition, the following day was the Science Fair at the elementary school, and Eli had come home from school declaring that this was the moment he had to have chemicals to make "slime" for his project. Charity was also insisting that she needed feathers as part of her demonstration on the difficulty of cleaning up oil spills. To make matters worse, Charity's flute lesson was at 4:00 P.M. As I dropped her off on my way to the store with Eli, she reminded me that she had practiced every day that week and that I needed to remember to get her the mint chocolate chip ice cream that was to be the reward I'd promised for consistent practice that week. She also reminded me for the twelfth time that, in addition to the feathers, she needed Jolly Ranchers candy to give as rewards for the children and parents who came to see her science exhibit the next day. I assured her that I would get everything.

I waved good-bye and whipped over to the grocery store, sent Eli to the specialty store for the slime chemicals and the feathers, and dashed around the supermarket like I was in a Laurel and Hardy movie in fast forward. Hoping that I wouldn't meet anybody I knew, I threw canned chicken, broccoli, mayo, and cream of chicken soup in the basket, to make some semblance of Jonah's favorite dinner—chicken divan. At the last second, I whizzed past the freezer case and luckily remembered the ice cream.

Eli had found the slime chemicals, but couldn't find any feathers. In desperation, I decided to slit open a feather pillow when I got home. By the time I threw the casserole in the oven and finished frosting the cake, I realized I was thirty minutes late to pick up Charity from her lesson. Richard was out of town and my other two possible drivers were unavailable. The party was in fifteen minutes and counting.

With visions of Charity crying on the curb, I broke the speed limit again and screeched into the driveway of the house where she takes flute lessons. I was relieved to see her looking happy. As she hopped in with excitement on her face, her first words were: "Did you get the Jolly Ranchers?" My relief turned to horror! Now what you have to understand here is that patience is not one of Charity's greatest gifts. She thinks that everything she wants is just as important as getting a mother in labor to the hospital before she has the baby in the car. When the look on my face told her that I didn't have them, she burst into tears and sputtered and wailed that she absolutely *had to have* those Jolly Ranchers! I tried to out-yell her ravings, telling her that I could get them in the morning before she had to set up her science project, and that she couldn't possibly know all the things I had to do in the next fifteen minutes. She continued howling and refusing to admit anything except that she didn't have what she needed . . . right now.

Suddenly, something happened. I snapped. It was like putting the jumper cables on the wrong bolts while trying to jump-start a car. There was a hiss and a sizzle and a flash of fireworks, like the giant burst of a Fourth of July sparkler. I screamed with the sort of uninhibited abandon I hadn't experienced since I was last on a roller coaster in high school. Before I realized what was coming out of my mouth, my eyes widened with rage and I yelled: "YOU CAN'T HAVE ANY JOLLY RANCHERS! YOU CAN'T HAVE ANY JOLLY RANCHERS! YOU ABSOLUTELY CANNOT HAVE ANY JOLLY RANCHERS." It scared me. I had really lost it.

The unusual desperation in my voice pulled Charity up short. She stopped her commotion and looked at me with amazement and horror, suddenly realizing that I had gone over the edge. Truly, her mother was the Wicked Witch of the West! I took advantage of the silence and loudly began to sputter out my frustrations. "Your unrelenting impatience is driving me over the wall. I can't stand listening to your constant demands for what you want. Life doesn't work that way. You have simply got to learn you can't have everything you want exactly when you want it!" I screamed. She started crying again, a little softer. By the time we got home, I was feeling ashamed of losing my cool. Even though I knew that my righteous indignation was justified and that what I had said was right and needed to be said, it was totally the wrong way to say it.

Still sniffling in the back seat, Charity looked destroyed. I began explaining to her my problems: earnestly, I told her about missing Jonah's concert, being late for the birthday dinner, and trying to remember everything. She actually became interested in my tale of woe. Reasoning worked. I told her I was sorry, and she forgave me. She told me she was sorry too. The birthday dinner was the shortest in family history, but it was okay. Jonah was late, too. No, I didn't plan to be a witch. But there are just times when I do a magnificent job of playing the part.

To me, the fascinating thing about motherhood is that it is truly a refiner's fire. Years ago, I had the opportunity to go through a pottery factory. There we saw beautiful creations in lovely earthen shades of clay, with graceful and varied shapes and curves, just before they went into the firing process. In fact, they were so lovely as they were that I asked a craftsman nearby, whose hands were the same color as the pot he was working on, why they need to be fired at all.

"Oh gosh," he replied, trying not to show his disdain for my ignorance, "if we didn't fire them, they would lose their durability and strength and fall apart very quickly. The least bump, not to mention time itself, would simply crumble them away. The firing makes the pots strong and durable and gives them a special luster inside and out." His eyes gleamed as he held up a fine example.

How true this is of motherhood! We start our mothering careers as rather ordinary-looking clay pots with varied shapes and curves—and march directly into the refiner's fire. The fire, however, is not a onetime process but an ongoing one. Every experience that helps us to be a little more compassionate, a little more patient, a little more understanding, is a burst of fire that refines us and leaves us a little more purified. The more we filter, strain, and purge through the experiences of our lives, the more refined we become. Of course, a fire can either give luster, depth, and strength, or it can burn and destroy. How well we use the heat is the key.

One summer I had an opportunity to meet several close friends whom I hadn't seen since high school and college roommate days, before any of us had children. Several children later, having been through not just childbirth but the everyday refiner's fire, these friends had a special luster . . . something indescribable and intangible and yet very real. That fire can make us more patient and understanding, able to handle near-impossible situations sometimes with grace, sometimes with disgrace, but always with added insight and understanding.

Looking back at the crises just described, I know that years ago, I would have fallen apart when I discovered that Jonah had not given us any notice on the time or date of his concert, or taken a total guilt trip that we had procrastinated in preparing the science projects. After years of refining, I've learned to handle a ton of interruptions, disappointments, and frustrations before I fall apart. Yet crumble I still do. But through the fire of experience, I also have learned to forgive myself and say I'm sorry, and actually to be glad for the added wisdom and insight into the next witch attack.

Just as I continue to be surprised that those visions of motherhood described at the beginning of this chapter did not turn out as I had planned, the best part is that reality is actually *better*. B. H. Roberts, a wonderful philosopher, said it well: "There is no progression in passing from ease to ease." My children make me be a better person—sometimes against my will. And the struggle with witchhood is part of the deal. I can't say that I rejoice in my afflictions, but I wouldn't give them back for all the witch's brew in the world. Motherhood is the greatest joy of my life!

Surprise Two

Childbirth Is Both Worse and Better
Than in the Movies

This last time in the delivery room felt almost like a movie. Trembling with excitement and fear and frantic anticipation, knowing that this would probably be my last performance, I hunkered down for the last few minutes of one of life's most astounding experiences: bringing a child into the world. Doctors and nurses, anesthesiologist and husband tightened the huddle around my little delivery table. Like the crowd at the Super Bowl when their favorite team is about to score the winning touchdown, they commanded urgently, "Push! *Push!* HARDER! PUSH!"

"Stupid crowd," I thought. "They've never even been in the game!" In exquisite pain, with neck veins bulging and eyes about to roll down my cheeks, I knew that the climax of Samuel Barber's *Adagio for Strings* would be a perfect accompaniment to the drama about to unfold. Even though in agony, I could feel the ecstasy of a spectacular sunrise about to burst forth as I watched in the overhead mirror that ninth bluish bundle of humanity begin to emerge into the world. Everyone in the room held their breath as we witnessed a miracle in progress. First the head, then another push for the shoulders, and then suddenly arms, bottom, and legs slithered into the hands of our experienced doctor.

Knowing that our last four deliveries had produced boys, he announced with almost childlike glee, "It's a girl!" His voice held the astonishment of one who has just witnessed his first miracle instead of the thousandth.

The relieved chatter of the "cheerleaders" and the hustle of the medical procedures fade into oblivion as the bustling room switches in my mind to slow motion. A fresh new spirit is gently placed on my abdomen. At last I can touch with adoring hands the personification of my nine months of wild imaginings. For a few moments, all that exists in the world is this new child and I.

Looking into the eyes of a newborn is a profoundly moving and spiritual experience. Heavenly harps and a choir of angels singing high extraterrestrial "ahs" heralding the birth of this new light take over in my head. I feel myself being sucked into eternity through those eyes, those dark pools of light that glow from an intelligence so fresh from a Heavenly presence. It is as though she is not looking at me, but through me to something or someone I cannot see. Maybe bidding a fond farewell to friends on "the other side," while this new body experiences life on earth—a new life. I remember Wordsworth's lines:

> Our birth is but a sleep and a forgetting:
> The Soul that rises with us, our life's Star,
> Hath had elsewhere its setting,
> And cometh from afar,
> Not in entire forgetfulness,
> And not in utter nakedness,
> But trailing clouds of glory do we come
> From God, who is our home:
> Heaven lies about us in our infancy!

She began to squirm and fuss, and I couldn't help thinking that this very wise, very old spirit must be very uncomfortable all squashed up inside this tiny body. Besides, she was wet and the world was cold. The music stopped and I whispered, "Welcome to the world," as they whisked her off to a warm bath and necessary arrangements for living.

Late that night after visits from an adoring Daddy with ecstatic siblings, I lay in a quiet hospital room with tiny new Charity swaddled in a white flannel blanket and firmly planted on my chest, her little fist tightly grasping a strand of my hair. There she stayed almost twenty-four hours a day for the next three days, as I knew that I'd have to stand in line to hold her when I got home.

Something about thinking that this could be our last child sent me flying through our eight other trips to the hospital. Saren, our oldest child, was born in 1970. Smiling to myself, I remembered that by the time I hobbled into the hospital for the second time that day, my pains were not like anything our Lamaze classes had described. From the book's calculations, I should be able to control the pain by breathing slowly and then more quickly, according to the intensity of the pain. Theoretically, I was to stay relaxed and comfortable without anesthesia.

On a scale of 1–10, the incessant pains leapt from 1 to 10 before I could even gasp, and stayed at that exquisite level for a full minute. If pain could kill, I was sure I would be dead. "Give me anything you have for pain and lots of it *fast!*" I pleaded in a way that would have made my Lamaze teacher ashamed to say she knew me.

Not much later, the astonished nursing staff, who were now the ones who were frantic, agreed that I was about to deliver a baby, and of course insisted that I move from one stretcher to the next during the height of a massive contraction. This seemed about as logical to me as asking a prisoner in a torture chamber to walk out and get the next prisoner just after having his feet chopped off.

On the delivery table, having cast modesty to the wind, I felt angry because none of the attempts at anesthesia had worked. I was frightened beyond words because I knew by now that for certain there was only one way out for this strange little individual who had been thrashing about inside the "big bump" for the past several months. And that way at that moment seemed unthinkable. Secretly I committed *never* to do this again!

Each successive time I could tell a similar story with variations on this same theme. Twice the anesthesia actually worked. Once, after a massive hemorrhage, I was rushed to the hospital for an emergency Caesarean section with a placenta previa, and went through the wild experience of having our tiny three-pounder born nine weeks early while we were living in London. On the second delivery, I foolishly waited a little too long to head for the hospital; plus we had to stop and get gas on the way. When I announced to Richard that he was going to have to stop the car on the freeway and deliver this baby, he put the pedal to the metal instead, claiming that he didn't know how to deliver babies. We flew in the emergency entrance just in time for the doctor to catch the baby as she made her grand entry.

With delivery number seven, we watched the baby's heartbeat disappear on the monitor with every contraction and felt so lucky to have little Noah when we found at delivery that his umbilical cord was wrapped around his neck three times.

Yet each unique delivery brought that child with those wonderful eyes and with the same Heavenly gaze that whispered somebody magnificent was inside.

As time passes, however, each child manages to bring the real world into focus. Little hands pat, pat, pat everything in sight and grasp supporting fingers like a gymnast on the bars. Little feet do their clumsy tap dance, and chubby toes and soles are tickled and squeezed and cuddled by the hour. Little cheeks are kissed so many times that it seems they should wear away from sheer erosion. Little mouths taste-test everything from funny-looking toys to Daddy's chin.

Time passes and things begin to change. Those eyes begin to focus and like to be open and observing more than we'd like them to be during the night and wee hours of the morning when we'd rather be sleeping . . . and less than we'd like them to be during the day, when we're trying to get something done. As those eyes get older, they begin to see things differently. They sleep too long when we'd rather have them getting things done, and often don't see why they should practice or why homework is so important.

Those sweet, adorable hands become the hands of a two-year-old unraveling thousands of yards of toilet paper a week, dropping sticky red lollipops on the new white carpet, writing on the walls with permanent Magic Markers; and they have even been known to hit siblings. Those same cuddly little feet track mud and snow on the car seat that you have to sit on, and often walk right into trouble.

As time passes, that same mouth that everything goes into as a tot learns to make the strangest things come out—things like, "You are the meanest mom in the world," "This food is *gross!*" and "Do I have to . . . like . . . go?" (These are the grungy moments that they don't usually show in the movies.)

Interestingly, the babies are not the only ones who change. We mothers change, too. The difficulty of everyday living sometimes brings out the witch that was hiding in the closet, which only appears when an angry ten-year-old accuses you of hiding the baseball mitt you have been trying to help him find, or when the four-year-old puts a pair of scissors through your new leather couch. For us, who whispered in that infant's ear that anything is possible—that they can do and be anything they dream they can be—it's sometimes hard to see the college president in the child who can't get his homework done (perhaps a little easier to see the absent-minded professor), the writer of a revolutionary new diet book in the child screaming under the table because she doesn't want to eat her peas, the marriage counselor in the child who is emotionally attached to his Power Rangers, and the magnanimous humanitarian servant in the child who won't share her toys.

The magnitude of motherhood and the great joy that it brings manifest themselves not hour after hour or month after month or year after year, but in individual moments. Drawn from my musings back to the quiet of the hospital room at 2:00 A.M., I realized that I was experiencing one of those moments as I watched this helpless, tiny new being enjoying mother's milk with one hand earnestly clasping my thumb and the other grasping my hospital gown as tightly as a mountain climber clinging to a rope . . . her only connection between life and death while rappelling down a steep cliff. I smiled and felt her cling desperately at first, then gradually relax as she sucked the nourishment she needed from one who felt blessed beyond words to have the privilege of providing it.

Hearing the sound of her gulps and watching her simple pleasure in "filling up" filled me with the wonder of where her paths in life would lead. The movie of *her* life flashed before me as I looked ahead and saw her graceful little feet doing pirouettes in pink ballet slippers and tutu, her excited hands holding on to her mortarboard at high school graduation, and her beaming smile, trembling with joy at the moment *her* first precious child is placed in her arms.

I knew through experience that this real-life movie which we were both about to undertake was going to be full of challenges and precarious situations, villains and heroes, joys and sorrows, but that it was much better than any Hollywood movie because it was for real . . . lasting and eternal. I knew it was worth all the money, time, sleepless nights, emotional upsets, physical stress, social dilemmas, and spiritual strugglings it takes to produce the greatest contribution to society: a loving, exciting, real life!

Surprise Three
Preschoolers Are Horrible and Adorable

Of the countless horror stories I have experienced at the grocery store with a toddler, my absolute favorite concerns a drama which a man observed at a neighborhood supermarket. As he entered the automatic glass door, he couldn't help noticing a young mother with a two-year-old who, before they even began her dreaded store odyssey, was already howling. He observed the patient-looking mother as she gently placed the child in the grocery cart, and overheard her saying, "Now, Jennifer, this isn't going to be so bad. We just have a few things to get today and then we'll be finished. Let's be calm, and everything will be all right."

For the next fifteen minutes, everyone in the store was painfully aware of where the mother and child were as the little two-year-old never quit her rantings and ravings. He saw the mother again at the dairy case with the child, still blubbering and insisting on something that she felt she had to have at that moment that was obviously unavailable. This time he heard the mother, who was now hyperventilating and trying her best to keep her emotions in check, say in a shaky but determined voice, "Jennifer, we only have three more things on our list and then we can be out in the nice, fresh air and we can breathe, and everything is going to be just fine!"

As he happened to be going out the door at the same moment as the hassled young mother, he couldn't resist catching up to her on her way out. With an understanding smile, he said, "Excuse me, but I just have to tell you how much I admire the way you talk to your child." The mother looked momentarily a little confused. Then, as though she suddenly realized what had happened, she smiled and replied, "Well, thank you, you're very kind, sir. But there is something you should know . . . *I* am Jennifer."

Is this not the way we all feel on certain days in dealing with preschoolers? "If I can just get through this next few hours, everything is going to be all right." We talk ourselves into survival. Just as surely as our kids are the delight of our lives with their daily new words and funny antics, and we feel that we must be blessed with the smartest little whippersnapper on the continent, we are also sure that we are going to be hyperventilating by the end of the day to survive until bedtime. (They are the very most adorable while they're sleeping.)

Difficult as preschoolers are, watching them as they observe the world is one of life's great pleasures. The world is so fresh and interesting to them. Anything is possible. One day when I had dashed into the Post Office, leaving four-year-old Noah with the sleeping baby in the car and assuring him that I would be right back, I got caught in a long waiting line. I rushed back to the car and was greeted with an anxious, "Why were you so *long?*" "I'm so sorry," I apologized. "There was a line in there." Immediately he forgot his impatience and his mouth dropped open in amazement. "There was a LION in the Post Office?" "No, honey," I giggled. "There was a big *line* in the Post Office." By now his big brown eyes were about to pop out of his head, "A BIG LION?" he exclaimed, as I rolled with laughter. In all fairness to Noah, there was a zoo across the street from the Post Office. A mental picture had flashed into his mind and he simply couldn't get it out. How wonderful to have such an imaginary sense of the real world!

Often we are entertained by misperceptions of things we assume these little ones know. Late one evening, three-year-old Shawni came running into the living room and plopped herself down by Richard. "Hey, Dad," she said, with her typical smile. "Let's pop our bags!" Trying to act intelligent, Richard just smiled and tried not to look too puzzled. "What do you mean by that, Shawni?" he asked cautiously. "You know . . . like you said last night, Let's pop our bags." It took several minutes for Richard to remember that the previous evening at bedtime he had said, "All right, Shawni, it's time to hit the sack!"

Preschoolers are also so absolutely honest. One day, Richard called to four-year-old Saydi, saying, "Where's Jonah?" (Our current "terrible two.") She yelled back without hesitation, "He's in the kitchen troubling up!" Sure enough, there was Jonah (whose greatest gift from day one was enthusiasm, and who sounded perfectly logical as he chattered away to himself, but sounded a lot like a tape recorder playing backwards to the rest of us) "troubling up" in the kitchen with those excited little fingers, opening every drawer and cupboard, vociferously exploring every pot and pan for something exciting to "invent." Just a few minutes before, he had been writing on the baby's face with permanent black Magic Marker. I guess he got tired of writing on the walls, the sheets, and his own tummy.

Speaking of permanent Magic Markers and preschoolers, one Christmas when Saydi was seven and the doll craze of that year was the precious Cabbage Patch Dolls, I had stood in line for hours waiting to get the real, bona fide, authentic Cabbage Patch Doll, complete with birth certificate, "given name," and official signature inconspicuously placed on the doll's bottom. On Christmas morning when Saydi put her "Jodie Mae" down for her first nap, three-year-old Talmadge, who had noticed us proudly displaying the "authentic signature" on the doll's bottom, decided it would be even more special if he put his signature there, too. In Saydi's mind things couldn't have been worse if World War III had just begun when she discovered the new "authentic signature." It took her years to forgive him.

Another similar ever present problem seemed to be children who wouldn't sleep through the night. People who tell me that their tiny infants sleep through on the first night home from the hospital make me feel sick. Although our first child was a good sleeper, instead of each child getting better, it seemed that we regressed and each child took a little longer to sleep through the night. I am sorry to tell those of you who are pulling out your hair to get an eight-month-old to sleep through that our last three children took about two and a half years to start. How well I remember those sleepless nights, being woken up every few hours with cries for bottles and pacifiers, and sometimes no special urge except the need to play . . . at 3:00 A.M. Those Dr. Spock no-no's of never propping a bottle or allowing pacifiers or even thumb sucking went right out the window after the first week without a good night's rest. I learned to prop the bottle in my sleep, and I even masking-taped a pacifier or two to a squawking little mouth. I've begged restless babies to suck their thumbs, often with no luck, and sometimes with such good luck that it took them years to withdraw from the habit.

By our last baby, when you'd think we'd have all the tricks of the trade ironed out, things were hopeless. After we had tried all the regular methods—not allowing an afternoon nap, not allowing a morning nap, begging, pleading, and reasoning—we decided it was time to let her cry herself to sleep . . . no matter what. Night after night we endured at least three hours with Charity screaming, Richard and I alternately holding the other one in bed and assuring ourselves that surely she was not being strangled by a burglar or devoured by a real monster. We thought *our* wills were strong until we met this little individual. One night, when she realized that screaming was absolutely not going to work on us, she started throwing up. She somehow knew that that would get us! Her will was like a guided missile. Throwing up worked for a while, until both Richard and I became so exhausted with the "cleanup" and the "stay up," that even that lost its effectiveness. Often we would hear her singing in her crib and we would know that she was peeling off every stitch of clothing. Even though we had tried every possible style of pajamas and clothes, thinking that there was no way she could get them off, somehow she always succeeded. After she got every stitch off, she would do a little dance, then wet on her blankets and start screaming for us again. In the end, we often gave up and she ended up in bed with us, thrashing about like the agitator on a washing machine for the rest of the night.

I remember staring at people who asked me to do things at the church or for the PTA during those hard years, which was also before I learned how to say no. I thought it would sound so ridiculous to say, "I can't do that because our two-year-old isn't sleeping at night." So I would reply, "Sure I'll do that," through clenched teeth, while thinking,

"You have no idea what you're asking of a woman who hasn't had any sleep for two years!"

One day, I took Charity with me to the mall (which I did in only absolute emergencies) because I was desperate for running shoes. She, in her typical fashion, rearranged several stacks of sweatshirts and a few of the shoe displays while I was alternately trying on shoes and trying to put displays back together. When the young salesman handed me the shoes and my receipt, he smiled at me and little fidgeting Charity at my side. "Good luck, lady," he said. "You're going to need these to keep up with her!" (For those of you who are struggling with these driven, type A children, they seem to be the ones who turn out to be the self-starters later in life: They get up and get dressed by themselves; they do their homework and turn in assignments on time—just a little strand of possibility for you to hang onto!)

I thought our preschoolers had invented every conceivable mess and disaster known to mother or father, but recently a man at a furniture store told me of one three-year-old's dastardly deed that ours hadn't thought of. He said one day his wife called him, sobbing hysterically. The only thing she could get out was, "How many chairs do we have in our house?" After assuring her that he really didn't know, maybe thirty in all, counting the couch cushions, she burst into a fresh round of tears and managed to tell him that their three-year-old son had just found the Exacto knife her husband had left out after wallpapering the night before, and without putting a scratch on himself, had cut a big X as far as his little hands could reach in the seat of every chair and cushion in the house. I guess I won't complain!

The greatest thing about preschool disasters is that—given time— they are also so funny. Some take more time than others to become funny. Some seem funny at the moment, while others may take you years to recover from, as in the gradual replacement of every chair in the house in the story just mentioned. (Luckily, the dad was in the furniture business!) But they do tend to wear you down. Those long nights of being up with nursing babies, then trying to be a pleasant, understanding mother the next morning when older children all seem to need something the other eighteen hours of the day, can make the years with preschoolers seem overwhelming and never-ending. We start asking ourselves, "What is *wrong* with me? Why can't I prevent these disasters? Why is it that these things always happen to me? It's got to be something I'm doing wrong!"

In actual fact, those horrible, adorable, tiny-kid frustrations and disasters happen to everybody. In fact, years of experience have taught me that rather than being surprised about disasters, we should actually expect them. I even progressed from rolling over in bed in the morning in the preschool days and thinking with dread and despair, "I wonder what will happen to me today," to waking up and smiling just a second before I open my eyes as I think, "I can't wait to see what will happen to me today." It took lots of kids and lots of hyperventilating and reassuring myself that I was going to survive the day. I finally figured out that life is a lot more fun if you determine in advance that it's going to be hard but you're going to try to actually enjoy the disaster and . . . chalk it up as a great story.

The truth is that the monstrosity of their deeds pales beside the joy that these little ones bring to our homes. Especially because as time goes on, we realize that preschoolers are tiny for just a minute and then they are gone. Even though you think you will never quit changing diapers, cleaning up messes, and pulling out your hair over a child's strange idiosyncrasies, it won't be long until you can't remember who threw a whole bushel of peaches one by one out the back window of the van on the freeway. Just remember the old saying, "When you get to the end of your rope, tie a knot and hang on!"

As inevitably as they do something that drives you to the brink, the next moment they come up with something adorable and endearing, often insightful, and even profound. It is those moments when you realize that something you have taught them has actually registered, and that they are now teaching you! Like four-year-old Shawni, who one day on a Daddy date while holding Richard's hand and tenderly patting it, said, "Now don't be sad, Daddy, because you know I love you, but I have to tell you that I think I love Jesus just a little bit more." Or three-year-old Saren, who, while being marched to her room after some sort of infraction, looked over her shoulder at me and said, "Mommy, when you get mad at me and put me in my room, just remember . . . I still love you."

Surprise Four
Your Mother's Role Is Bigger Than You Think

On a cold, wintry day in 1991, my mother came for a visit. Visits to our house during the school year are rare because the journey takes three hours on narrow, winding canyon roads, which are treacherous in winter—and winter seems to last most of the year in our neck of the woods.

So there was wild hugging in the kitchen when she arrived, as she was attacked by a gaggle of grandchildren. "Show and Tell" ensued as each child took a turn to show her the latest A+ on a Social Studies Unit, demonstrate a new remote-control car, haul her off to show last week's dance revue on video since she couldn't be there, and play the latest piano recital piece for her which she had heard only over the phone.

That night Richard had agreed to take all the children who didn't have prior commitments with him to a nearby city to autograph books and then on to a movie, so that Mother and I could have a little uninterrupted time together.

I relished this historic chance to spend an evening with her, sans husband and children. Rubbing my hands together, and knowing that she didn't get a chance very often to come the "big city," I said, "Well, Mother, what would you like to do tonight? Go to a nice restaurant and then see a good movie or a play?" I was ready to show her a really grand time.

She hesitated for just a moment, looked as though she was savoring the thought of our evening together, then said, "Could we go bowling?"

Now, that may sound funny to you . . . but what you don't realize is that my mother grew up at a time when it was very unpopular to be an athletic woman, yet she adored athletics of all kinds. She was the best broad jumper and high jumper in the county, and became one of the best woman basketball players in Wyoming. While all the other girls in high school were ogling at the boys, she was moving the piano out of the way in the old gym so that she could play basketball with the boys. She spent most of her life with bruises on her knees from diving for the ball. When she got too old to dive and jump and run, she took up bowling. At the present time she was the star of her Montpelier, Idaho, bowling team. Just a few weeks earlier, she had bowled 170! Richard makes it a point never to go bowling with her. It is so embarrassing to lose to your mother-in-law . . . especially when she is eighty-five years old!

Yes, that is not a misprint, folks. She was eighty-five and remembered, just as I was giggling about the request to go bowling, that the Jazz, her favorite NBA team, was going to be on TV that night. I knew that wild horses couldn't drag her away from that. She watched or listened to every game and knew almost every player on every NBA team nearly as well as our seven-year-old. She often insisted on driving long distances by herself rather than with friends so that she could listen to the games as she drove. Though we begged her to travel with her friends for safety's sake, she'd just say, "They're not interested in the games. They're just old people."

After watching the game that night, we played piano duets. When my mom wasn't playing basketball as a girl, she was playing the piano by ear in a dance band with several members of her family. Eventually she learned to read notes and studied piano extensively in college. She was determined that her children would experience the great satisfaction she had known through music. When violin teachers weren't available in our rural little town, we traveled ninety miles through a narrow canyon to a town where my sister and I took violin lessons every other week from a professor there. As a child, I spent thousands of hours with tears dripping through the piano keys or down into the F holes of my violin while she stood over me saying that I couldn't do anything with my friends until my practicing was finished. Not only that, she brazenly claimed, "Some day you'll thank me for this!"

So there I was—thanking her *again* for making me practice as we rollicked through some piano duets and played some of the old songs we used to play with my sister on the violin at almost every funeral and wedding reception in Bear Lake Valley.

Later in her life, after teaching thousands of piano lessons, influencing hundreds of children to love music, and working for forty years as a schoolteacher, where she convinced possibly another thousand that each was the best student she had ever known and so must work very hard, she was able to save enough money to purchase her pride and joy: an organ. A few years ago, she decided that it was silly for that organ to be enjoyed only by herself, as she was living on her own after the passing of my dad in 1979, so she had it moved to the rest home two blocks from her house. Now, at least once a week she thrills those capable of that emotion and brightens the lives of others as she entertains the folks she refers to as "the kids" at the rest home—most of whom are many years younger than she is—with her "old-time" favorites.

I had the distinct privilege of growing up on a farm. While Mom was giving lessons, Dad was milking cows; feeding chickens; raising sheep, cattle, pigs; and saddling horses. I don't ever remember going to the grocery store as a kid, as our little farm provided our own meat, milk, eggs, and a large vegetable garden. We canned fruit in the fall and my mother made bread every week. My sister Lenna and I churned butter on Saturday mornings while we watched *The Little Rascals* on TV and Mother taught piano lessons.

Occasionally my dad would bring several chickens home to be butchered, plucked, and cleaned. Dad would chop off their heads, and after the first time I watched them run around headless with blood spurting from their bodies, I couldn't eat chicken for about seven years. I distinctly remember telling my mother that I would clean the whole house, do all the dishes, and practice all day if she would just excuse me from the horror of pulling out the insides, plucking off the feathers, and scalding the carcasses to sanitize them. She agreed every time, but I remember her saying, "Now, Linda, how are you going to know what to do with chickens when you get married?" I assured her that I was going to marry somebody rich enough to buy me chicken already cleaned, plucked, and cut up! (And I did.)

In many ways, my childhood was idyllic, yet filled with the normal idiosyncrasies of any childhood. My father, who was a living, breathing saint, had married my mother when she was thirty-eight and he was fifty-one. He was of pioneer stock, and worked harder than any person I ever knew on the farm or at any hard labor job that would bring him a little money. With only eight years of formal education, he was also the wisest person I ever knew. He had been married previously and had had two children with a wife who died of cancer. When he and my mother married, they thought they were unable to bear children, and after three years they adopted a five-year-old son. Almost immediately I made my appearance, to their surprise and delight, and a year later my younger sister, Lenna, joined us. By then my dad was fifty-five and Mother was forty-two.

In a way, thinking back about living in those old childhood days seems as strange as thinking forward about living in a Star Wars movie. Almost everything in my life today is entirely different from what it was when I was a child. Yet, interestingly, the values that I retain that are good and consistent are the things that my parents taught me for those few years that I was living with them before I left for college, which then seemed like an eternity and now seem like a moment.

I wasn't lucky enough to inherit my mother's athletic genes. No matter how hard she tried, my mother could not give me her athletic ability. I am the klutz of the world. However, I can see her incredible athletic ability coming out in some of our children (with quite a little help from Richard). She did deliver to me, through her gene pool and her tenacity, an ability with music, which I value greatly. But the things that I value most are the things that she *showed* me through her example.

Sure, there were a few funny things that she taught me unintentionally, like how to slam a knife and fork drawer when she was angry. Whenever Mother was mad, we knew it because she would go into the kitchen and slam the drawer with the knives, forks, and spoons in it. (It was her sign of an oncoming witch attack.) This is something I swore I

would *never* do when I got married. As it turned out, I could hardly un-
pack our new silverware fast enough when we first arrived as newly-
weds in Boston, where Richard was to begin at the Harvard Business
School, to slam the drawer! I chuckle when I hear some of her little
"witch" episodes coming out of *my* mouth. Sometimes in the very same
words!

But, oh, what good things she showed me how to do—things like
never passing up someone in need, how to follow up on responsibilities, and how to work hard to get what I wanted. She showed me how
to look for needs, and that the kids my age who needed the most help
were usually either the quietest ones or the loudest ones.

I have failed many times in applying the principles that I learned
from her, but other times I feel that I used things she taught me in ways
that neither of us could have possibly imagined. Now I see many of
both my parents' great qualities cropping up in our children as I watch
them finding the good in each person and the importance of the ethic
of hard work. Every person is unique and very special to my mother,
whether a homeless vagabond, whom she would gladly hire to fix her
roof, or one of her own grandchildren. I think every grandchild secretly
thinks that she/he is her favorite. Through her, they have learned to be
tolerant and loving and generous. My humble little widowed mother
just can't give her hard-earned money away fast enough to anyone in
need, from our own struggling college-student grandchildren to a family down on its luck. "It's so much fun giving money away," she claims.
"What else would I do with it, anyway?"

The influence of good parents and especially in this case a good
mother (because of the nature of this book) goes much farther than any
of us can possibly know. Our mother's role in our life carries on for generations. The older our children get, the more I see her in them. It
makes me wonder how I am like my mother's grandmother, who also
had an influence on me, though I never knew her. I know that some of
the things she taught her daughter, who in turn taught *her* daughter,
are part of me. It is an awesome thought to wonder what my great-
grandchildren will be contributing to their families because of me. The
frightening thing about your influence as a mother is that the long-
term effects for both good and bad may be eternal.

True, many people have not had the opportunity to have a noble mother or even to know their mother. Drugs, alcohol, depression, and sometimes death can make it impossible for some to know the real soul of our mothers. This can affect people in one of two ways: It can destroy their ability to function well; or it can give them strength to break the vicious cycle and do something much different with their own children. Lessons learned from bad experiences can make them stronger and more able to cope with their own children, so that they can make a brighter future for them. In this case, perhaps they can become a mother who stands out as a beacon who changed the course of the history of that family. I know this sounds easy—especially coming from someone whose harshest childhood memory of her mother was that she couldn't stop slamming the kitchen drawer. But I did have a half brother who died an alcoholic, a half sister who left a young family to struggle after she died of cancer at forty-one, and an adopted brother with severe problems from being abused as a child. I feel the importance of turning families around, even in very difficult situations. I have seen, firsthand, the devastation of dysfunctional families.

This autumn we will celebrate Mother's ninetieth birthday. In the past five years she has endured two falls, resulting both times in a broken pelvis and deep depression, which necessitated medications that are toxic to her both physically and emotionally. We all know much better the meaning of enduring to the end than we did just a few short years ago. Yet she is indefatigable. She has with true grit and determination been able to extract herself from all the medications, and now talks like she's sixty-five again. She's not quite ready to bowl yet, but she's back playing the organ at the rest home and rendering many hours a week of service extracting names of ancestors from microfilm. I'm not sure how well she can see, and we have to repeat things sometimes, even with her hearing aid; but her sense of humor thrives, and she continues to teach us daily about service and patience and endurance and never giving up. Some day we'll thank her for that, too!

"One more year, though," she says, "and I'll be ready to go!"

Surprise Five
Getting Work Done at Home Is a Myth

"Well, this is going to be a snap!" I thought, as Richard drove off with four children one summer weekend and left me with only five. I was dying to get to the work I'd been procrastinating doing for weeks, and was convinced that with only five children to work around, I was going to be able to accomplish miracles.

I had stayed up the night before until 1:20 A.M. critiquing Richard's new book draft and had promised myself an early night tonight, since I was going to get all my work done during the day. "I've simply got to quit this staying up until the wee hours of the morning," I determined resolutely. "This afternoon I'm knocking out the rest of Richard's book and writing two articles for the newsletter while the children play."

We were on an extended stay at our little mountain lake cabin in Idaho. Afternoon came and I found a pen (which wasn't easy) for a child who wanted to write a story, set lunch fixings out for everyone and told them to help themselves, then sneaked to the back porch where the kids seldom lurked, manuscript and notepad in hand, and began. I got through almost a page before nine-year-old Noah found me. He came out with his own pen and paper, dragged a chair over next to mine, and said, "I really need help with this story I'm writing. I just don't know what to say next."

Before I could even answer, I heard four-year-old Charity yelling, "Mommy, Mommy, *where are you?*"

"She's out here!" Noah screamed in his classic bullhorn voice before I could clap my hand over his mouth, and she gaily skipped out the door to my side.

I began eating the cashews that were on the table, feeling guilty about every nut, having just committed—again—to a low-fat diet.

"What time is Dad coming home?" Charity chirped. "And when are we going back home?"

"Four days," I said as tersely as possible while reading my manuscript, hoping that she would get the idea that I was busy and go away.

No such luck! How long is four days, anyway, she wondered, completely oblivious to my dilemma. "How many *minutes?*"

Just then Noah dropped his pen and it rolled to a crack on the redwood deck and plopped through. "Oops," he giggled. "Do you have another pen?"

By then seven-year-old Eli had discovered us and came out to ask for some watermelon. At that moment thirteen-year-old Jonah opened the back door, pulling his own easy chair in one hand and a journal in the other, thinking he'd also found a great place to write. He passed by Eli, his favorite child to tease, and said, "Why do you always wear dirty shirts?" As always, Eli burst into tears.

"Since Dad is gone, can you take us water-skiing tomorrow?" Jonah asked, completely ignoring Eli's wails as though it was a job well done.

Just then the phone rang. It was Richard, telling me that some people I didn't know were coming to play tennis with me tomorrow. I reminded him that I didn't really *play* tennis, which he said didn't really matter. "Humph! Doesn't matter to *whom*," I thought as I cleaned up the watermelon mess and looked for another pen for Noah. I finally resorted to my best fountain pen and returned to my "secret" hiding place complete with five kids. Sixteen-year-old Josh had joined us to have a few cashews.

"Get these cashews away from me!" I pleaded, and kindly asked everyone to leave so that I could work. No one made a move. Charity continued as though she had never been interrupted.

"When will I be seven?" she inquired.

"Three years," I said as tersely as possible.

"No, I mean how many *days*," she said, totally disgusted that I hadn't thought to tell her that in the first place.

At that moment, Eli let out a sharp scream and yelled, "Jonah hit me in the shoulder for nothing!"

I tried to work that one out, but I must admit I was pretty tired from staying up the night before and exasperated by then, and wasn't a bit nice about helping them sort it out.

The instant there was a "free space" after the reconciliation, Charity piped up again. "When did Grampa get born and who is his mother, anyway?"

I would have admitted that the situation was getting ridiculous in any case, but just then Noah said, "Mother, I have to tell you the truth about something! You are going to kill me."

"What is it, Noah?" I asked, a little alarmed. "Come on, you can tell me." After fifteen seconds of hesitation, he said, "You're not going to believe this, but I dropped your good pen and it rolled into the *same* crack. I'm sorry!" he groaned, looking like a silly sheep.

We just all had to laugh. It was simply outrageous. I explained to them that I really had a lot to do and would love it if they could all please leave me alone for just one hour. No one moved. There were several moments of silence, then Charity broke it by saying, "Do napkins grow on trees?"

Suddenly I remembered why I always stay up so late. On the spot, I vowed to forget the manuscript and articles (but not the cashews) and try to get all questions answered and dilemmas solved by at least 11:00 P.M. so that I could then begin.

I also promised myself to quit being surprised that getting office work done during kids' waking hours is a myth!

Surprise Six

The Practice
of Patience Is Perpetual

Almost the universal response when I tell people that I now have nine children is, "My, you must have a lot of patience!" A list of the few good attributes that I did have at the time I began having children definitely did not include patience.

It took many years of struggling with my need to be patient, along with my desire and ability to have patience, to realize a simple fact: Patience is a learned skill—just as playing the piano is a learned skill.

Many people say, "I'd love to play the piano!" but when it comes right down to it, they don't have enough desire to learn to spend the hundreds of hours of practice necessary to play well enough for it to be useful. So goes patience.

It is true that some are born with natural gifts for music or patience, which makes things much easier; but most of us have to "slug it out." We must have a burning desire, and then plan and visualize, work and practice, until we actually become better "players."

It is easy for psychologists and philosophers and husbands to say, "Change your habits. Be patient and understanding. Just don't raise your voice!" But the intricacies involved in remaining calm as a mother are unimaginable unless you are a mother.

The last time I lost my patience, which was yesterday afternoon, I found the experience frustrating and embarrassing. At the beginning of a Cub Scout meeting, I received a long-distance call from someone who needed help. With a crying baby on my legs, I tried to talk on the telephone while the Cub Scouts used the newly cleaned couch for a trampoline. A pillow fight ensued (our couch includes about twenty pillows). After I finished the call, I found that the baby had discovered the artists' chalks and had scattered them on the floor upon which the Cubs had thrown pillows and were jumping and sliding. Green and black oil-based chalk was all over our couch and our new, light beige wool carpet. Next, our twelve-year-old, whom I had just taken to the junior high to find her lost English papers which she was frantic about, was whining about not being able to have an ice cream bar even though Josh just had one. Of course, my wrath was showered on Josh, who at that moment had descended to the bottom of the stairs. Half an hour earlier he had *promised*—after begging for five minutes for an ice cream bar and reluctantly (after three "no's") receiving consent—that he would not let anyone see him eating it.

Pointing my finger at him, I said in a very loud, exasperated voice, "Josh, you may *never, never, never* again have an ice cream bar after school."

"But, Mom," he began.

"Just don't ever ask me again," I raved on, not letting him say another word. "I told you this would happen. I knew it! Now everyone's begging for ice cream."

I drew in my breath to finish, and he managed to get a word in. "Mom, I just wanted to tell you that Matthew's mom is here with his things."

I died when I looked up, finger still pointed in wrath at Josh, to see Matthew's mom smiling down at me! Red-faced, I stammered hopelessly and tried to explain my actions as we both giggled a little amidst the whoops of Cub Scouts (luckily, she's a mother, too). Nevertheless, I was embarrassed at doing exactly what I promised myself I would not do.

Having already confessed to witchhood several times, I know that my progress to patience is very slow. I do think it helps, however, to have the following six guidelines in mind as we practice patience.

1. *Don't overvalue material things.* When you buy something new, predetermine that the chances are more than fifty-fifty that it will soon be dented, smashed, crushed, written on, spilled on, or scratched! Although it's wise to caution children and to do all you can to preserve your nice things, there's no reason to be reduced to a screaming bundle of nerves over things. Feelings are more important.

I'll never forget an incident when Noah was five years old: He accidentally swept a new bone-china bowl off the bar and onto the floor, where it smashed into a thousand pieces. Richard, who had just carried that bowl by hand all the way back from England, was furious and sent Noah to his room. Fifteen minutes later Noah reemerged, with swollen red eyes but still a little belligerent. With his hands on his hips he loudly inquired, "Dad, which is the most important, the bowl or me?"

2. *Visualize yourself as the "calm center of the storm."* Before you "hit the troops" each morning, go into the bathroom, look in the mirror, and spend two minutes meditating about the events of the day. I personally don't have to guess whether or not there will be a crisis. I'm certain of it. Visualize walking into "hurricane" situations, and determine that no matter what happens, you are going to remain "the eye," the calm center of the storm. Actually go through little dialogues in your mind of anticipated scenarios. Rehearse your lines. I've found that this actually works—about 35 percent of the time to begin with, but the percentage gets better with persistence. Which is better than nothing!

3. *Set reachable goals.* Instead of setting the goal of being patient with all of your children, try to concentrate on being calm with one child at a time, especially the one who is most exasperating. There will still be times when you lose your patience, but be willing to forgive yourself. You're only human. Explain your anger to

your children when you get mad at them, and ask them to forgive you. Let them know you're human, too!

4. *Don't lose your control when your child says, "That isn't fair!"* Calmly remind him that life isn't fair, so he'd better get used to it. Let them know that the circumstances cannot always be the very same for every child. Our older children are already panicked about how spoiled Charity is going to be. We remind them that that is what youngest children are for!

5. *Use a still voice of perfect mildness.* Christ set the perfect example of calmness. His voice has been described as "a still voice of perfect mildness." Whether you realize it or not, the tone of your voice sets the mood for your household. Try a fun experiment. Memorize the following statement: "Overwhelm them with calmness." It's a mental concept that can be brought about physically *sometimes*. You'll be amazed at how much it helps if you can call that phrase to mind whenever things get frantic and your patience is taxed to the limit.

6. *Decide on calmness in advance.* Chart your impatience for a week. Every time you get angry, write down why. You'll probably discover some interesting things. Maybe you consistently get angry because your two-year-old is a walking wave of destruction or your ten-year-old is always late or your twelve-year-old still whines. Write down (a) what bothers you; and (b) how you react to each situation. Next, realize that one of those two things has to change. Premeditate and practice a new response to irritating behavior. For example, say, "I'd like to help you feel good about being on time. How can I help?" instead of, "The car pool's waiting again! I just can't believe that you can't put your shoes where they belong so that you won't always be late for school!"

One Sunday, I made the following chart for four of my children. It may help you see what I mean and enable you apply it to your own situation.

Child	Problem	My Reaction	Plan for Better Action
JONAH	Won't mind first time	Total exasperation and often anger	Establish special reward for minding without being reminded
SHAWNI	Always has little aches and pains	I give her the feeling that I don't want to hear about it and don't believe her	Grit your teeth and show real sympathy
JOSH	Won't get up	I yell down the stairs and tell him to get up so many times that I get blue in the face and furious	Give him his own alarm clock, then let him be late a few times and take the consequences
SAREN	Worries about ridiculous things and won't be consoled	I expect her to accept my "easy" solution, then get caught up in an argument when she won't agree	Treat worries seriously. Offer alternate solutions, then change the subject

Use the principles of deciding in advance particularly at those predictable high-tension times of the day. In our home, those times are in the early morning before school, and when the children get home from school. Concentrate on ways to make such times smoother.

Even as I review these guidelines, I find that I still lash out at an unsuspecting child and lose my cool regularly. But I can also smile through a few more disasters every year and have found that practice makes patience!

Surprise Seven
Children Fail; and So Do Mothers.
Or, Will Herman and I
Ever Amount to Anything?

This is a good day to write this chapter because I am depressed! I'm not talking about the chemical or hormone imbalance kind of depression. (I am pregnant again, so I guess that accounts for some of it.) What I'm talking about is the kind of depression that comes from banging your head against the wall after trying every conceivable reward, bribe, and punishment in the book, and a lot that aren't, and still being unable to motivate a child to get things done—to perform according to reasonable expectations. Having just talked about patience, we all realize that there is usually one child who continually pushes it to the limit.

At the moment, Herman is my problem. (The name has been changed to protect the not-so-innocent.) This curly-headed, cherubic-looking, blond twelve-year-old is about to drive me up the wall. It is Herman's job to empty the dishwasher, but the dishwasher is always full! Herman's siblings get twenty-five cents for every article of clothing of Herman's (or anyone else's) that they pick up and put away; the fine comes out of Herman's hard-earned money. Yet there is always a pile of clothing on the floor in front of his drawers. Herman gets paid according to how much he practices, how often he makes his bed and cleans his room, and how consistently he does his household jobs. Unfortunately, Herman is getting poorer every week.

Herman often forgets his homework—or waits until the last possible minute to do it. He has also been known to forget to take it back even when he gets it done. When his teacher asks him for his work, he honestly can't remember whether he did it or not! Sometimes he finds it crumpled up at the back of his desk.

Since Herman has to buy his own clothes, he has a limited supply of clothing. (Thank heaven for birthdays and Christmas, or this child would be absolutely destitute!) This morning when he went to his room to get ready for school, he found his clothes had nearly all disappeared. And what he could find in his drawers was dirty. (He can't keep the hamper separated in his mind from his drawers.) Now, Herman has gone to school before in dirty clothes, out of absolute necessity, but these were unthinkable!

"You empty the dishwasher," I said when I saw his frantic face, "and I'll find you something to wear."

Five minutes later when he came downstairs from his room, I said, "Herman, it's your practice time, so throw on these sweatpants and this sweatshirt and get to it."

Having just turned twelve may have made Herman realize that he could no longer wear sweatpants with holes in the knees to school. He just couldn't. Amidst his tears and some unflattering remarks from me, we found some new birthday pants, six inches too long, tucked them under, and pinned them with the last four straight pins in the house. (Safety pins are nonexistent five minutes after I buy a new package.)

Just then, the car pool arrived early, and I was horrified to see that all three of my boys' hair looked like it had been blown dry while they were standing on their heads. As usual, "Mr. Nobody" had taken every brush and comb in the house, even the ones I'd carefully tied to the bathroom sink. (It doesn't take long to untie a knot in an emergency.) In desperation, I grabbed the nearest toothbrush and "toothbrushed" the boys' hair as they shot out the door.

I put my head in my hands as they drove off—and in the same motion, looked down to see the dishwasher. I simply could not believe that it was still full of dishes! I was so angry at this child who could not seem to do *anything* right that I decided at that moment that I was going to go to the sixth-grade room, interrupt whatever lesson they were having, take dear Herman by the hand, and announce to the class that I was taking him to unload the dishwasher!

"Maybe Herman is mentally deficient," I thought, as I shook my head and mourned the clothes on the floor in his room, the bed not made, the trumpet not touched.

Contemplating what I should do with this "problem child," my mind drifted back to a conversation I'd had with my good friend Margaret, a mother of seven boys, living almost without a husband for the last six months while he began a new job in another state.

Since our families were similar in size and age, we had talked on the phone only two days before to corroborate and commiserate. I remembered a story that she told me. "Last week I got so exasperated with Jason, I thought I was going to die," she said. "The school bus was in front of the house and I went dashing up the stairs screaming, 'Jason, Jason, you're late!' I found him sitting at his computer, working on an intriguing new program, in another world, still in his pajamas, totally unaware of where he was, what time it was, or probably even *who* he was. Furious, I shouted at him to get ready fast and that I would take him. I was especially angry because now *I* had to get ready, get my preschooler ready, and make the round trip to the junior high school, which took forty-five minutes, which meant I would be late for my morning meeting. Totally miffed, I proceeded to yell at him all the way to the school. Jason didn't have a chance to get a word in edgewise. 'You are never going to amount to anything if you can't get your act together and get where you are supposed to be on time,' I raved. 'I can't believe I have such an irresponsible child!'

"I reached the height of my righteous indignation as Jason got out of the car at the school with a discouraged look on his face. He didn't say a word, but just as he was about to shut the door, little three-year-old Anthony, who had been listening from the back seat, jumped up from his perch, leaned over the front seat, looked straight up into his big brother's face, and loudly proclaimed, in his sweet, sing-songy voice, 'Jason, I love you!'

"That poignant moment took my by surprise. Tears came to my eyes and I felt like such a fool," she went on. "If it hadn't been for cute little

Anthony, Jason would have gone to school feeling stupid and unloved! Here I was, the mother who had vowed to be the best mother in the world, always positive and caring, and I had almost sent my son—who I was only temporarily disappointed in—to school feeling stupid and unloved. 'Oh, I love you too, Jason,' I blurted through my tears. 'More than you'll ever know!'"

I was shaken from my thoughts by the phone ringing. It was Herman, who said rather timidly, "Mom, you know the crepe paper we bought last night for Mrs. Ellison's birthday party. I was in such a hurry this morning that I forgot it."

"At least he remembered he forgot it before the party," I thought. I knew he was happily surprised when I said, "I'll bring it right down. I'll meet you in front of the school," without the least hint of irritation in my voice.

As I hurried to get ready to leave, the only toothbrush I could find was the one I had brushed the boys' hair with. I couldn't find my purse, which I had just a few minutes before absent-mindedly laid down somewhere. "If Herman is mentally deficient," I thought, "it's because he's related to me!"

As I drove to the school, I remembered that a few days before, Richard had staged a little "halfway-through-the-pregnancy party" for me by buying me a cute sweater (it was for a skinny person—but someday it'll fit) and a video (which I didn't have time to watch). It was a truly moving gesture. Late that night, after bedtime, Herman came to me with a little brown lunch bag folded over. "I'm sorry I couldn't find anything better for your halfway-through-the-pregnancy party, Mom, but this was the best I could do." In the bag was one of his new pencils and a pencil sharpener, which I had seen the day before amidst the mess under his bed! I hugged him and was sure at that moment that he was going to amount to something wonderful.

This morning as I handed Herman the crepe paper at school, I grabbed the hand that reached out for the package and I looked straight into his face and said, "Herman, I love you. I really do—even if you didn't empty the dishwasher." (I couldn't resist that one little reminder.) But I said it with a smile. He smiled back with a sheepish grin and that satisfied look that only comes when you know your mother loves you, and skipped back into the school with one leg of his trousers dragging on the ground. At that moment I realized how much I loved that child, and was horrified at how near I had come to squelching his self-esteem. A child's soul is so delicate and easily crushable. As trying as they are at times, they are like precious flowers that need to be constantly nourished.

Ah! Just having written this down makes me feel so much better and forces me to realize some days are like that. Children come with their own personalities. Some are freer spirits than others and some think in different patterns than I do.

We should never give up teaching them correct principles, but we have to allow them to be themselves in applying those principles to their own lives. Progress takes more time for some children than others. Remembering this, even though some children seem to be living in another world, may help us realize that their world may in fact be better than ours.

Surprise Eight
Dissonance and Sibling Rivalry
Are Facts of Life

For some reason, the thing that delights people most when Richard and I talk to them about parenting is to hear that we fight. Because we often talk so much about ways to improve family life, we have to be very careful to let audiences and even friends and neighbors know that life is just as crazy at our house as it is at theirs. We see other families' smiles at church on Sunday or at family picnics or beaming at us from family pictures and assume that things are as they seem in those picture-perfect moments all the time. I keep shaking my head and saying, "If the people who think we are perfect could just see this!" I *love* going into someone else's messy house. It makes me feel so much better about my own! When we did the Oprah Winfrey Show with six of our children, talking about our book *Teaching Your Children Values*, the audience asked where the other three children were and we told them that they were doing humanitarian service and missionary work in Europe. We all giggled when Oprah said that they were probably hoping they were in a drug rehab center somewhere. Funny, but true. Many people would probably feel some satisfaction if one of our kids turned into the Texas chainsaw murderer. Although it isn't that bad, we do have consistent terrible moments.

Several years ago Richard ran for governor in our state, which was a truly grueling experience. The children and I left early from a large convention where Richard had been speaking because we were all exhausted from day after day of campaigning and always needing to be cordial, look good and at our best. On the courtyard outside as we slipped away, I had six tired, hungry children following behind me like ducklings. Suddenly one "accidentally-on-purpose" stepped on another's foot, and a full-fledged yelling fight ensued. Tired, hungry, irritable, and laden with problems myself, I snapped out a nasty correction and tried to find out who started it and why.

Not far behind us, two men whom I was glad I didn't recognize were closing in on us fast. I quickly tried to smooth things over, embarrassed by every child who had chimed in on the argument, and not very happy with myself either.

The two men quickened their pace and my heart sank as I realized that they recognized us (which is one of the distinct disadvantages of a family whose dad is running for office). "Well, if it isn't Linda Eyre," one of them blurted out with a big smile on his face. "You've just made my day!" he chuckled, as I stumbled over the niceties amidst stillgrowling children. One had actually gone off to sulk. "My wife will be thrilled to know that the Eyre kids fight too!"

I giggled and felt my face blazing. It was funny, but I was mostly mortified that anyone would think the Eyres don't fight. Please know . . . it's a promise . . . *we fight!*

Johann Sebastian Bach, one of my favorite composers, also teaches great lessons for life through his music. He used many methods to make his compositions moving and creative, one of which was *dissonance*. Over and over again, through passing tones and intentional "wrong" notes, he created a brief, uneasy feeling. Most interesting of all was the relief he could make the listener feel through the *resolution* of the dissonance.

Bach was a master at resolving the dissonance in his music in wonderful ways—sometimes in predictable ways; other times in creative new ways. A man known for his "well-tempered clavichord" in turn taught me a lot about the tempers at our house. I hope you heave a sigh of relief as you realize that dissonance is necessary to contrast with and resolve into harmony. Dissonance actually makes life more interesting. It helps us grow and progress. The important thing is how we resolve the dissonance. If we do it right, a feeling of even more harmony results, whereas the wrong resolution can cause even greater feelings of anxiety.

Think of a recent example of dissonance in your home and decide whether that dissonance was resolved to create harmony or more dissonance.

As you read the following example from our house, notice that it sometimes takes a little compromise and accommodation to turn dissonance into harmony:

I shouldn't have been surprised when eight-year-old Saydi asked if her friend could sleep overnight again this weekend, but I blurted out the resolution without reservation. "No way!" I said emphatically, while hurrying to finish the dishes so I wouldn't have to spend all morning in the kitchen cleaning up after the kids left for school.

"Why not?" she pleaded.

"You had Jenny over last weekend. You stayed up all night, kept your sister awake with your giggling, and were a grizzly bear all the next day. I'm amazed that you would even dare ask."

"But Amy and I are best friends. We hardly ever get a long chance to be together. Either she has a violin lesson after school or I have piano. I just don't see why we can't. Please, Mom, p-l-e-a-s-e!"

Saydi is your basic, great actress. Her pleading voice took on a sense of urgency, pain, panic. "I have to have a sleepover," she wailed, as tears began plopping off her cheeks like a leaky faucet.

But I remembered my resolve from last week. "Absolutely not," I responded coldly. "I don't want to hear any more about it. Go do your practicing!"

With a fiery exit she yelled on her way down the stairs—hoping I would and wouldn't hear her at the same moment—"I never knew you could be so *mean!*"

As the "feathers settled," I knew I had made the right decision, but I just didn't feel right about it. There was a distinct discomfort lingering in the air. I realized that my method of resolution was not good. Deciding to look at the world through her eyes for a few minutes, I thought about how much she wanted to be with her friend. That little friend was someone who didn't demand anything from Saydi or judge her, who didn't make her feel like a little sister or expect her to be perfect. Maybe she did need her—but not all night.

Just as the children were ready to walk out the door for school, I called Saydi aside. "Why don't we have Amy come over after school and play and have dinner with us and then play again. That would give you girls lots of time to be together. Then about seven-thirty, we'll take her home so you can both get a good night's rest. How does that sound?"

After a big unsolicited kiss and hug, Saydi skipped off to school looking as though the weight of the world had been lifted from her shoulders: a much happier resolution, resulting in even greater harmony.

Dissonance is a part of life. Whether it's only a passing note or a big, out-of-shape chord, we need to expect it, even anticipate it, and sometimes think about resolutions in advance. Other times, we just need to keep working at it until it feels right. Remember: Interesting dissonance makes for greater harmony!

I wish I could say that we have found the great, golden key to stopping sibling rivalry forever at our house, but I can't. I've decided that sibling rivalry in various stages of intensity is part of living in a household which has more than one child.

Last night on a three-hour trip in the van, I determined to make a list of all the rivalry that occurred during the journey home. It was late, and all ten kids (our nine plus a friend) were tired. For one fleeting moment I worried that they would just go to sleep and leave me without any good material. What a joke!

We started out with little things like, "Jonah is pinching me through the crack in the seat," and "Move your foot, Saren. It's in my hair." By the end of the journey, we had one major battle between an eleven-year-old and two teenagers. The younger sister swore that they had awakened her on purpose, and the older girls were pleading innocence but insisted that she deserved to be awakened because she was taking all the room. Another scream emerged from the back as Josh wailed that his eyeball was scratched because Shawni had kicked him with her shoe. The dramatics were amazing. I quit keeping track after the first ten rivalries and decided simply to summarize.

On the day-to-day basis, despite the fact that it doesn't stop sibling rivalry, we have found one method that really helps kids to work things out themselves. When two children engage in a battle, they are requested to sit on what we call the "repenting bench," which actually is a place to repent. In our house, it is a short, uncomfortable wooden bench just big enough for two. Squabbling children are sent immediately to this repenting bench, where they must sit until they can tell Richard or me what they did wrong. Of course, it's very easy for a child to know what the *other* child did wrong. If they get tired of sitting or can't figure out what they did wrong, they ask the other child to tell them because the other one *always* knows. We try to emphasize that "it takes two to tangle," and that even those who plead complete innocence need to realize that it was partly their fault.

Next, we ask them to go through a little dialogue. If the children can say, "I'm sorry. Will you forgive me? I'll never do it again," with some semblance of sincerity, and give each other a hug, they are allowed to leave the bench. True, it may take a little time for one child to decide whether or not he or she is going to forgive, and sometimes the exercise is just a way to get off the bench, but somehow that little exchange of words and the physical touching almost always work wonders. (Maybe they're pretty good at it because they get so much practice!)

Don't plan on this working perfectly the first time. You need to role-play this with your children before the actual fight occurs and realize that it works best with younger children. Your sixteen-year-old may require a different system. However, it does take you out of the position of referee, deciding who's right and who's wrong. You're always wrong. It puts the resolution of arguments in the children's hands. Working things out as they happen also keeps the air clear. Deep sibling rivalries can last a lifetime and be deeply scarring.

One day when I was doing a radio call-in show on sibling rivalry, the first caller was a man who had been driving on the freeway and had pulled off and found a pay phone so that he could tell his story.

His family consisted of his parents, himself, and one brother. At an early age he was labeled as the good boy and his brother as the bad boy. When the boys grew, the labels began to take hold, and he remembers a great deal of rivalry between them. However, as an adult, he gained a deep love for his brother and established a good relationship with him as long as the parents were not present. Whenever they returned to the picture, the rivalry reared its ugly head. There were so many things that had never been worked out among them. Confiding in us, he said that his brother had died an alcoholic and that he was still having severe guilt feelings about their rivalry.

His call made me realize that sibling rivalries are not only irritating, troublesome, exhausting, and disruptive, but can also have devastating long-term effects if they are not handled well. Just those sometimes perfunctory sessions on that repenting bench can do wonders to keep long-term bad feelings between children from building up, and begin to establish friends for life as your own children become adults.

Another thing that helps our family handle sibling rivalry is to talk a lot about "What would Jesus do?" Whether or not you are Christian, you have to agree that Jesus' personality was totally noncombative. He always returned good for evil, love for hatred, compassion for intolerance. Often, after our children are involved in an argument, we ask them to role-play the argument again, and this time to try to think what Jesus would do: i.e., return a hug for a hit, an "I love you" for an "I hate you." Just the other day when two children were fighting vehemently over who should have the "shotgun" seat in the van, I asked them to consider what Jesus would do if His brother wanted that seat. Next, they proceeded to get into a more friendly fight, each insisting that the other should have the seat. Sometimes you just can't win!

Here's a story that will help you feel a little better about the rivalry going on in your house. One night a very prestigious man from our church came for dinner. We respected him greatly and wanted to have our children have a chance to spend an evening with him. But the kids were all little, and by the end of the evening Richard and I were totally embarrassed. We just assumed that they would be well mannered and polite in the presence of such an important man. To our amazement, they often seemed to forget that he was even there, fighting over who took too many potatoes and who had got their way about what music we should be listening to during dinner. (We could not imagine how these two mild-mannered, opinionless parents had produced such strong-willed children.) One disagreement after another broke out all evening.

As our honored guest was leaving, we apologized for the behavior of our strong-willed children. He smiled and graciously said something that I will never forget. "If you're going to raise leaders," he said, "you've got to expect them to have a will of their own. I know it's hard to deal with, but just be glad that they have an opinion!"

Sometimes, as illustrated so beautifully by Bach, dissonance is a way to produce more harmony. Expressing strong opinions isn't always a bad thing and in fact can lead to really good things . . . if you can just survive today. Hang in there!

Surprise Nine
Witches Live with Warlocks

The dictionary says that a warlock is the male equivalent of a witch. However, there are two definitions of a witch: (1) An ugly and ill-tempered old woman; and (2) a bewitching or *fascinating* woman (or man, in the case of a warlock). I definitely believe that I sometimes qualify for the first definition and Richard usually fits better into the second.

I think that "fascinating" is a perfect word to describe Richard. I met him when I was a sophomore in college. A roommate and I had decided that we were going to have absolutely nothing to do with marriage for many years. Determined to see the world together—study abroad, get a Eurorail pass, and go everywhere and do everything we'd ever wanted to do—we had made a pact to stick together until we were twenty-eight. Then we would settle down and get married.

I met Richard on a blind date under circumstances too complicated and funny to explain here. We ended up talking long into the night about life and what we planned to do with it. By the time I got home at 2:00 A.M., I was mortified. I shook my beloved roommate Lorraine to her senses and told her that I was so sorry and so upset, but I had just found the person I was going to marry. We both cried.

I guess Richard liked me too, because he continued asking me out (although I don't think that marriage had occurred to him). In fact, he wanted me to break every date I had and go out with him every time he wanted me to. I said absolutely not, and decided that he was too insensitive and with great relief, I told Lorraine that I was mistaken. We didn't have to worry after all. Richard and I dated off and on for two years. I went back to the Europe plan, but got caught up in responsibilities in several organizations at the university and never made it. When he was a senior, Richard went off to New Hampshire to work for George Romney's campaign. When Romney dropped out, he changed to Nelson Rockefeller's campaign. When he lost, too, Richard came back and graduated with straight A's, even though he hadn't even been in class most of the year. "Hm, there must be something to this guy after all," I thought.

After that first date, during the time that most romancing couples spend making out, Richard and I spent arguing. We each had iron wills, and of course, each felt that he/she was always right. Richard was usually calm and rational, and I was emotional and irrational (and usually the one who was *really* right).

Still, I found him fascinating. He had big plans to attend Harvard Business School and be part of the solution to society's problems. Excitement and pizzazz were always part of our dating experience. He was desperately poor, and so was I, but he always found ways to have fun without money. I wouldn't really call him cheap, but I don't think he ever spent more than fifty cents on any date. (He will deny that.) When we weren't arguing, we had a splendid amount of fun. Actually, even the arguing was fun—especially the making up part. I began to love him for his mind. He loved me for my body . . . just kidding. But after telling him twice to bug off, I decided that my first impression was inspiration and that I should marry him. After two years, we were sure we were meant to be together for eternity.

We had fun getting engaged, fun being engaged, and fun getting married. Actually, it has been fun *being* married, too. Four days after the wedding, we packed everything we owned in our two cars. I had an old spaceship-looking Ford Galaxy and he had an old red bathtub Porsche. (Did I say he never spent any money? Actually only on things that were *investments*. I don't know where that puts me, but anyway . . .) We drove across the country for our honeymoon. It was about Iowa that I decided to tell him that I could eat my own Big Mac all by myself. I had been giving him my other half during our courtship because I knew he was still hungry and I wanted to be dainty. But I was starving.

We began our married life in Boston. It was here I realized that I could be a pretty nifty witch (as described in the first dictionary definition, ill-tempered, etc.). I also realized that Richard was not only a good thinker, a good money manager, a great friend and lover, but he was also an extremely fascinating warlock (as described in the second definition).

The way he made beds was particularly fascinating. The agreement in our house was that the last one out of the bed makes it. But when Richard makes the bed, he can make it look as though I'm still in it. The way he does the dishes also fascinates me. From that first week in our little student apartment, he insisted on doing his share of the dishes. It was a loving and noble gesture, but after months of doing the dishes over again, I gently tried to dissuade him. "This is a family tradition," he pronounced. Those were the old days before we had a dishwasher. When that convenience came along, I thought things would get better. But alas, every time he stacked them, the dishes came out with little bits of food plastered all over them like bugs on a car grill after a long summer drive.

It was also fascinating to me to find that Richard loves to eat a fourth meal every night at about 11:00 P.M., indiscriminately using up all the leftovers and messing up the kitchen. The biggest problem is that he likes to eat it in bed! "How can you make turkey casserole sound like celery," I complain as I roll over with a moan, my stomach rumbling from my new diet. Smelling and hearing him eat are positively bewitching. The worst part is that after he finishes, he absolutely *has* to floss his teeth. Plugging my ears just doesn't help a bit!

If there is such a thing as a child warlock, Richard would also qualify. He doesn't like the rest of us to do anything without him. When I registered for a ballet class with our two teenage daughters, he thought he would like to join the class, too, much to the horror of the girls. He also has more strange ailments than all the kids put together. While claiming to have the body of an eighteen-year-old, hardly a week passes without a weird headache or side ache or debilitating ingrown toenail.

My warlock still blooms. Fascinating Richard finds it hilarious that I cannot figure out anything having to do with electronics. Every time I go downstairs to exercise while I watch TV (which isn't often), somebody has messed up the cable in the back of the TV while setting up the video machine or Super Nintendo. The mass of cables, end holes, and switches behind the TV totally befuddles me. One day while trying to help me, Richard tried unsuccessfully to hide his frustration as he was late for a meeting. "I just can't see why you don't get this," he muttered absently as he deftly pulled cables, switched switches, and screwed in joints.

That night as I lay exhausted on the bed at midnight, I asked Richard if he would please put the wet clothes in the washer into the dryer and turn it on. "Sure," he said, with just a little hesitancy. Five minutes later, he came back up and sheepishly asked, "How do you turn on the dryer?" I told him. Several minutes later, he came back up again and said, "I'm sorry, but I just can't figure it out."

After I turned on the dryer and we'd snuggled up for the night, I said in the darkness, "Don't you find it interesting that I can't figure out how to turn on the TV and you can't figure out how to turn on the dryer?" I could hear him smile.

For every weird thing I didn't know about Richard, there are forty wonderful things that I couldn't have known in my wildest dreams. To name them would take too long; I'll reserve that for another book.

Almost every "witch" has a "warlock" to live with. Yet I have a hunch that working out the differences will be one of the most rigorous and interesting things we do in life, especially if we realize that the goal is not living happily ever after, but struggling and learning as we strive for real oneness in spite of our witchhood and warlockness.

Surprise Ten
Teenagers Are Like Werewolves

When I was a teenager, I really loved werewolf movies. I think one of the reasons was that the people who turned into werewolves were always such nice people. When the moon came up, they would suddenly sprout long, hideous fangs, and straggly, gross hair would pop out on their arms and face like alfalfa sprouts growing in fast motion. Wild, piercing, glowing eyes would tell us all that they were really no longer themselves, but had been taken over by some supernatural power that would cause uncontrollable harm to everyone and everything in their path. The part I like the best, though, was that in the morning, when the moon had set, these wild creatures turned back into wonderful people, with torn clothes and dirt under their fingernails, wondering what on earth had happened to them.

Does this not sound strangely like the description of a teenager?

For twelve years I looked forward to our children becoming teenagers with dread. Every time someone saw us struggling with our little brood, they would smile at us and say, "Just wait until they're teenagers!" They said it with the inflection of their voice at the end of the sentence—instead of rising in anticipation—dropping with a sound of dread. I admit, I was scared.

I had been apprehensive about each new age our children entered into. When I was pregnant, I used to wonder what on earth I would do with a baby. Even though that turned out to be somewhat manageable, I had the same worries about terrible two-year-olds, and then I wondered what I could possibly do with a ten-year-old boy. Now here we were, about to dive into the teenage years.

But like it or not, into the teenage years we plunged. We have now had seven teenagers over the past twelve years. We've had either four or five teenagers at once for six straight years and we have ten years of living with teenagers still to go. You may be interested in our findings so far. Someone once said to me, "Take a good look at your child when he is twelve, because about the next year, he will become a strange, new person for nearly seven years. By the time they turn twenty, you may get that sweet twelve-year-old personality back." There are some elements of truth to that supposition, but pleasantly we have found it not to be entirely accurate . . . yet.

Yes, we have had many sleepless nights wondering where our teenagers were, sure they were dead on the road somewhere and hadn't yet been found. Indeed, they are as strong-willed as we are. Many heated discussions have passed our lips about curfews, video parties after midnight, and generally how to do things. (Disturbingly, teenagers often have undebatable logic and are often, yes often, even right!) Yes, we have had teenagers who think they're dumb when they're really smart, ugly when they're really beautiful, and sad when they are really happy. The phone is usually an extension of their ears. They can't understand why they have to do family things so often, as they would really rather live with their friends. They often wonder how they ever deserved such a wicked witch and wary warlock for parents. And they know everything about almost everything.

It's true, teenagers *are* like werewolves in terms of how wide their mood swings can be. But usually they turn back to their real selves within a few days, a couple of hours, or sometimes even within minutes.

Once, for a Junior Prom, Saydi had this grandiose idea of having her hair and nails done. After hours of instruction and "re-instruction" to a hairdresser who redid her hair after the first time failed to meet her expectations, and having some funky fake nails put on, she came home in a panic with rollers still in her hair and blowing on her nails, as her date was arriving in twenty minutes. She insisted that only she could take out the rollers. To our horror, when she unveiled the hairdo like someone taking the bandages off after plastic surgery, she looked like a cartoon character who had been electrocuted. Not only that, several of her lovely pink nails slid off to the side of her fingers and the polish was crinkled. She had a brief werewolf attack. Her eyes were just like those of the werewolves in the movies as she shrieked, "Oh no! What am I going to do! I *can't* go like *THIS!*" We looked at each other in disbelief. As she gazed, dazed, into the mirror, two big tears popped out on her cheeks. Then, suddenly, she snapped out of it as she was attacked by her sense of humor. She began to laugh hysterically. It was just too funny to be true. We laughed until we cried. She survived.

The apex of the teenage years for me is when these crazy werewolves get their driver's license. By hook or by crook, they always manage to get their driver's training completed and persuade us to take them to take their tests on the very day they turn sixteen. When it was time for our first child to get her driver's license, I was counting the days like a three-year-old does until Christmas. At the time, I was escorting our children to twenty-two different activities during the week—including eight basketball games, violin, piano, cello, and harp lessons, and soccer practices and basketball games. Just as I could feel the day of my salvation at hand, I went out to drive with Saren before she took her test. To my horror, I realized that she was a terrible driver. I knew I wouldn't feel comfortable even knowing that she was driving a stray dog to the dog pound, let alone her siblings to soccer practice. Luckily, she flunked the driving test.

In fact, we are famous at our house for flunking the driver's test. When Jonah turned sixteen, he was given a big sendoff by family and friends as we proceeded to the Driver's License Division. For months, he had been counting down the days. At last he would be free of constantly looking for rides to hockey practice and frantically asking for earlier rides home to meet the family curfew. He could not wait to be at my beck and call and run every little errand and car-pool for me. (Those of you who have teenage drivers know that this lasts for about three months. Then they become much too busy just getting themselves where they have to be. Getting someone else somewhere becomes very rare.)

He passed the written test with flying colors. But the huge colorful grin on his face as he left for the road test had changed to ashen gray as he walked in the door fifteen minutes later. Horror of horrors . . . the worst possible scenario had come to pass: He had flunked the road test. The moon was up! The world had ended! Two more weeks with a learner's permit driving with an *adult!* An eternity. I could see the fangs popping out as he knew he could never survive.

"I can't believe he flunked me!" he howled. (At sixteen, Jonah already had enough body hair to qualify as a werewolf.) "I only did a couple of little things wrong!" he raged. After a long, scary silence I dared to say, "What happened?"

"Well, I did start out on the wrong side of the road," he admitted. "But I got right back over when I noticed it! And I didn't notice the red light at the railroad crossing. But it was just a fake course. I *know* I would have seen it in real life!" By the time he got home, he was sure he was also flunking out of school, that he had no friends, and that he was surely going to die!

Ah, the resilience of youth! He did pretty much stay in the werewolf mode for two days. But by the end of the two weeks, when he went back to retake the test, the moon had set, his fangs had long since disappeared, and he was chuckling about what a good story this would be to tell his kids.

When it came to our next teenager, Talmadge's turn to take the test, Charity—who was eight at the time—had prepared a special poster for Tal's birthday party. She figured she'd present it to him at the family party after he'd taken the test. It said: "Happy Birthday Talmadge CÓN-GRATS!" with an easy way to mark out the C-O-N-G in case he flunked so that it would instead read: "Happy Birthday Talmadge . . . RATS!" Luckily, he passed the first time.

The one who really should have flunked was Saydi. Within the first few hours of getting her driver's license, she had hit a stationary hay wagon parked on the side of the road. She was driving my new car, loaded with friends who were jostled but not hurt. Within five days, she also hit a rain grate on the side of the road in our old van and popped two tires and bent both the rims. (Ask us how you tow a van with two flat tires and two bent rims on the same side.) Now at nineteen, she still has the nerve to giggle and remind us that she *did* pass the test the first time!

On a more serious note, sometimes you have to almost lose a teenager to realize how much you really love them. Last year we came within an inch of losing Jonah. On a spring morning, as he ran across the crosswalk to the high school at 6:30 A.M., he was hit by a car going at 40 mph. I believe that a guardian angel or somebody from heaven intervened and saved his life as he flew through the windshield and landed in a sweet Hawaiian lady's lap. The good news is that his head, neck, spine, and arms were miraculously spared and in perfect order, with the exception of one tiny bone chip out of his left shoulder and five stitches over his eye. The bad news was that both legs were severely damaged from the direct hit by the bumper of the car. The bones of his right leg were jutting out of the skin, and three of the four ligaments in his left knee were completely shredded. He was pretty well out of commission for the next six months. We learned to love that teenager immensely during that time as we saw him go through surgery after surgery, have screws inserted, and get sewn back together. He spent his time going from hospital bed to wheelchair to crutches. As painful as it was to watch, we observed that during that seventeenth year of his life, Jonah almost completely outgrew his "werewolfhood." Nearly losing your life makes you grow up in a hurry!

There are two main things that I have learned about teenagers. First, that teenagers are not just one big lump of the same kind of trouble. Their personalities are just as different as teenagers as they were as toddlers. Some have masses of friends who fill our house to capacity. (After a basketball game last winter, we had a spontaneous "cereal party" with fifty-seven of our oldest teenager's friends "chowing down" on the bags of cereal from our cupboard. Actually, I think it's cheaper than pizza, and luckily, I buy cereal by the bag.) Others feel more comfortable with two or three close friends. Some are sensible and others are silly. Usually they choose admirable friends, but some are "interesting." Sometimes they are reliable, and other times, pretty flaky. Some are voluminous daters and others are so frightened of rejection that they don't dare ask. Some are opulent optimists and others are perpetual pessimists. Some have a crisis a minute and others are unruffled by anything. I'm so grateful for the perspective of having several teenagers to help me figure out that they're not weird, they're just themselves. Not only that, they have taught me so much about myself.

The best thing that I've learned about teenagers is that, werewolves or not, they are my favorite age to live with. Their delightful love for life, mixed with those daily crises and heated debates, makes life interesting. We have just graduated our fifth child from high school. They have somehow survived all the werewolf attacks and have their feet firmly planted on the ground. We look back with a sigh and a smile at all those high school days filled with Junior Proms, Senior Assassinations (this is another story), even car accidents, and staying up all night to help with an English assignment. As I write, I look at a picture of one of the seniors on an a capella trip to California, and see a huge group of glowing, happy teenagers. Our own is front and center. (Have you noticed how your own child usually looks like the star in those group pictures?) "Those were the days!" I think. Thank goodness we've still got some more coming.

If, for you, teenagers seem like something in the far distant future, get ready to have fun . . . seriously. And if your teenagers are already becoming werewolves and driving you crazy, enjoy it while it lasts because you blink . . . and it's over!

Christmas Makes You Realize
with Real Eyes

Whether your favorite holiday is Christmas or Hanukkah or Thanksgiving, let's be honest: Holidays produce stress. So often we fail to see the real meaning of the holiday because we get wrapped up in the "trimmings and wrappings" instead of seeing the real benefits. I call it "realizing with real eyes" the meaning of what we are actually doing. Because in our family we celebrate Christmas, I am addressing that holiday specifically, but what we are saying can apply to any important and elaborate holiday.

One of my worst problems at Christmastime is not being able to find the time for my "real eyes." Every Christmas I vow that I'm going to get organized sooner by having all my presents bought by December 1. I commit myself to quit accepting assignments to take special treats to the fourth grade when I don't even have time to make Christmas cookies with my own children, and resolve that I'm going to quit worrying about what clever new things to take to the neighbors. None of which I do with much success. Last year I began feeling that I was on a merry-go-round and couldn't get off. I heard several mothers say, "I hate Christmas. It is really the low point of my year." I must admit that I have had that very thought cross my mind, and have felt myself becoming a "witch" at the very time I should have been an "angel."

Endless lists of gifts for relatives, friends, and neighbors—not to mention being Santa Claus's little helper, cookie dough and cake batter spilled down the cupboard doors, endless rolls of Scotch tape, paper, and ribbon, holiday open houses to attend, and being in attendance at every child's Christmas concert—often made me an irritable grump instead of a happy camper. The list of "things to do" becomes overwhelming and depressing.

Even the mail, which is plentiful and fun to read if you can find the time, can be depressing as you read about all your friend's "perfect" children and their amazing accomplishments for the year. Last Christmas I read one "Christmas letter to friends" that was absolutely incredible. The accomplishments of each of eight children got more and more amazing. Knowing what it took to produce children like that, my eyes were bugging out by the time I finished reading. It went like this (the names have been changed to protect the innocent):

Dear Loved Ones and Friends,

This year has been a wonderful one at our house. Jennifer simply loved her study-abroad experience. She absolutely inhaled the sights and sounds of ancient and modern Europe. She had a starring role in *Camelot* and still finds time to sing in vocal groups, play in the civic symphony, and hold down a part-time job.

Alex graduated from Viewmont High School as a student body officer and attended Boys' State. He recently received his Eagle Scout Award. He'll be touring with a dance company next summer, playing his banjo with a live band.

Jan is an excellent student. This year she resumed her study of piano (along with mandolin and cello). She is on the tennis team and also excels in softball and basketball.

Joseph started high school this fall and has participated in many school and community plays. He has been to Disneyland this year twice (with choir and Youth Symphony). He is great at cutting hair and was chosen as sophomore "Preferred Man."

Elizabeth has scads of friends who call her every minute to see if she's still breathing. She's a great baby-sitter and is developing her talents in violin and clogging. She is repulsed by modern music and much prefers the "oldies" radio station.

Allison is in the finals for the third-grade Knowledge Bowl team. She takes lessons in piano and clog dancing. She's also in the University Children's Dance Program.

Louise is dramatic and artistic, is continually cutting, pasting, and sewing, participated with her brother in the Children's Chorus for *The Nutcracker,* and studies clogging and modern dance.

Our baby, Kelly, is a joy! She has a wonderful imagination and makes up names for everything she has and can play alone for long periods of time with only tiny toys and her imagination.

We love you all—Merry Christmas!

My reaction was to look up and say, "This is sick!" How can one family possibly do all this? How could one mother possibly get all those kids to all those places? The human nature in me rationalized that they must be working with a very different gene pool than ours! Of course, I realized that this dear mother, whom I do love and admire, was only mentioning all the very *best* things that had happened to her children rather than the things that were driving her crazy. It made me think that some Christmas, just for fun I'd like to send out a Christmas card with a form letter that presented life at our house with *real* eyes. It would go something like this (the names have been changed to protect the guilty):

Dear Friends and Those of You Willing to Admit We're Family,

We've had a hard year this year. Let us tell you about it.

Joseph procrastinates until it drives us up the wall. He's always screeching in at the last second making or missing deadlines by a hair.

Sarah is "Miss Sweetness and Light" to her friends, but mostly cries and whines about how far behind she is and how tired she is when she's at home. Her room is always a *disaster!*

Julie never has good, reliable friends. She always feels betrayed and left out, and can't think of one good thing to say about the world on those days.

Harry made a deal with us that if he got a 4.0 GPA, he could quit piano lessons. We made the deal and to our amazement, he did get straight A's for the first time in his life! (Actually the joke was on him because we were about to make him quit piano anyway. After three years of lessons he's still not sure which way is up and which is down on the keyboard.)

Amy shops till she drops and then gets home and decides to take everything back. We can't believe that she is also over-spending her budget after all the financial training we've given her.

Jeremy would rather die than do his homework, and often actually forgets it on purpose. He has to be taken by the hand and "sat by" to keep him on track.

Tom cannot stand to lose an argument and is incapable of stopping his mouth before he gets himself in trouble. He misses the bus at least twice a week.

Max has a terrible temper, is a perfectionist, and consistently runs away from home. (I help him pack.)

And our sweet baby Susie runs the household. She's a disaster a minute. We swore we'd never spoil a child, but I guess that's what youngest children are for. When she says, "Jump!" We say, "How high?"

P.S. At least four of our nine children have not yet learned to flush the toilet. We're not certain who because of the predominance of "Mr. Nobody" around our house.

We hope things are a little better at your house. We love you all—Merry Christmas!

With tongue firmly planted in cheek, I must say that getting a letter like that would really make my day. Sometimes it looks so much like everybody else has got it together and we wonder what is wrong with us . . . until we realize the simple truth: we're just normal.

I have found that a little mind-searching to simplify and get perspective helps you see what's important with "real eyes" during the holiday season. Here are some suggestions:

1. Close your eyes and visualize what you want for your family at Christmastime. Dream about traditions that would make your Christmas more memorable and sort them out from the ones that make it a hassle. Be brave enough to lovingly tell your parents that it's time to start your own Christmas traditions on Christmas Eve, Christmas morning, or whatever, instead of being at a huge family party—if that is what you really want.

2. Write down a list of all the things that you would like to do at Christmas. Then mark each one with a VI (very important), SI (sort of important), or TD (trivial details). Plan exactly when to do the VIs. Fit the SIs in if you can; and forget the TDs.

3. Have a brunch after the opening of the gifts on Christmas morning (something simple but nice) instead of spending the rest of the day preparing a huge Christmas dinner (unless that is your favorite thing about Christmas), and *you* get to play with the kids' toys or watch the football game all afternoon, too!

4. Realize that some Christmases are more elaborate than others, depending on your financial situation and the arrival and disposition of new babies and two-year-olds. Enjoy the differences instead of begrudging them.

5. Instead of worrying about what to give to the person who has everything, and trudging all over town to find something appropriate, give a priceless gift—something from your heart—a written tribute.

6. Learn how to say no gracefully but with firmness and conviction. Also, be ready to offer alternate suggestions, e.g., instead of making gingerbread houses for each of the kids in your Sunday School class, give them a candy cane and a little note of appreciation; or better yet, take them to deliver goods to a needy family.

7. Limit kids' Santa Claus lists to one major gift (cruel parents). Let them realize that it is not their option to ask for everything their hearts desire. You can fill in things from Mom and Dad that you want them to have or can reasonably give them.

8. Shop early and wrap presents as soon as you purchase them, so that you can enjoy the nativity play by the children on Christmas Eve and ponder the real meaning of Christmas without being preoccupied with the drudgery of staying up all night to wrap gifts. Save the assembly of toys for older children who can help on Christmas morning. Part of the excitement can be putting it together.

9. Make it a tradition to do something truly service-oriented, instead of getting caught up in making new decorations for the tree every year. Ideas can range from taking dinner to the elderly to making a lovely Christmas for a needy family whose children will go without if you don't provide.

10. We love the example set by our neighbors who took their children to Mexico for Christmas. They had planned to sit in the sun, but when it rained for two days, they decided to go to the village orphanage and see what was needed. They had their most memorable Christmas ever as they bought gifts for each little child in the orphanage and personally presented them. They had made their own pact not to receive one single gift for themselves. Now that our children are older, and we have lots of free airline miles from so much traveling, we have started having our Christmas a day early with our traditional fun food and *one* small gift, and then traveling to Hawaii for Christmas. It gives us so much more time to think about our Christmas service projects and to concentrate on what Christmas is all about. Christmas without massive gifts has come to mean something totally new and different. Hawaii may be "a bit far" for most families, but spending time away anywhere with the family can make Christmas exciting again.

All frustrations aside, there is something magic about Christmas. For us, the magic happens when we discover the real meaning of Christmas by trying to do what Jesus Himself would do if He were here to help. Our family's best Christmas memories are the ones we spent under the viaduct downtown, serving breakfast to the homeless, or the "Sub for Santa" year when we found a mother with seven little boys whose husband was out of state looking for work as she struggled to put food on the table. Another Christmas, one of our daughters and her friends picked a down-and-out teenager to befriend at the high school. They pooled their meager money and came up with enough to buy a really nice shirt at The Gap. They also gave up some nice clothes that they weren't using and wrapped them beautifully. Richard got to be the lucky "Santa" (who he didn't know from Adam) who delivered the "anonymous goods" to the boy's door. With secret smiles, those kids enjoyed watching this boy proudly wearing his new clothes all year.

You can make Christmas what it is supposed to be. Turn your visualizations of a happy, stress-reduced celebration into reality. Regardless of what the media and your friends and children tell you, you're in charge of Christmas at your house. It is so much fun to put the joy back into Christmas!

A dear friend named Gordon who is single and on his own at Christmas shared with us his way of seeing the season with "real eyes." (This is one of my all-time favorite Christmas stories.) As a single man with quite substantial financial resources, he felt a strong need to help other single men who were less fortunate than he. He thought he'd like to invite a couple of homeless men from the transients' shelter to have Christmas Eve dinner with him. When he got to the shelter, he was filled with compassion as he looked over the many faces seemingly lacking all hope, and decided to invite everybody. All forty of them! He and a girlfriend had such fun spending countless hours shopping for and preparing a turkey dinner with all the trimmings to share with these homeless men. His father, who thought he was crazy, said, "Well, Gordon, if you have to do this, for heaven's sake, don't put out your sterling!" Gordon thought it over carefully and decided to put out his very best—the best china, crystal, *and* sterling. When the time for the dinner party arrived, he had all forty men picked up in taxis and brought to his home, where they enjoyed a delicious holiday meal. In addition, he encouraged each man to make one long-distance phone call to loved ones who might be concerned about him, especially during the Christmas season. When the party was over, there were many expressions of thanks. But one man hung around until the last taxi had arrived, seemingly drinking in the marvelous refinement of a beautiful warm home, the exquisite Christmas decorations, and the wonderful food. Many thanks were handed out that evening, but Gordon will never forget the one from this last man to leave. Having been quite emotional all evening, the man turned to Gordon just before he got into the taxi. Holding his face in his hands, he looked straight into Gordon's eyes and said, tears spilling down his cheeks, "Now I know what Jesus looks like!"

May we all begin to see Christmas with more real eyes!

Surprise Twelve
"Learning Disabilities" Can Be a Great Gift

I knew that there was something special about this child. From the moment he emerged from his own private but cramped swimming pool to the harsh light and sounds of this world, sucking on his first knuckle with those beautiful dark eyes and calm, I-can-handle-this, demeanor, I knew. We called him Talmadge, but the nickname that stuck was "Tam-the-Lamb."

One particular morning, six years later, "the Lamb" was late for school for the third time that week. This little first grader obviously needed to learn to hurry! Babbling all the way to the school about getting up earlier and getting ready faster, I screeched to a halt at the bottom of the school steps. As he put his hand on the door handle to get out, he turned to me and said, "Mom, did you notice how the sun reflected off the water in that manhole cover back there?"

My mouth dropped and I remembered again as I looked into those now bright blue eyes and at those adorable buck teeth from sucking on that knuckle all those years that I was looking at someone much older and wiser than six. Sorry that I couldn't be more like him and live more often in his world of naturally noticing beauty and angles and color, I smiled at him and promised I'd look for it on the way home. "Okay," he said, with a little parting advice: "Mom, put on your seat belt."

Meanwhile his teachers were telling us that Talmadge was not reading on grade level. I could see that he was struggling. He had no interest in letters and numbers. Initially we were not particularly worried, as we had had several older children who had not found reading easy, had gone for extra tutoring from our wonderful resource teacher, and were now all doing very well on grade level and some even above grade level.

But our little lamb was different. He continued to struggle in school—with teachers saying that he was behind, not handing in assignments, often in a world of his own. By fourth grade, he was spending most of his day in the resource room or laying with his head on his desk in the classroom complaining of splitting headaches. Every time we suggested testing, he would react with horror, insisting that there was nothing wrong and that he could do better.

I started reading books about learning disabilities in children, watching what was happening at home and at school on a daily basis, talking to his lovely, supportive classroom teacher, talking to resource teachers, and taking him to the hospital for physical therapy for his headaches. Resource teachers said that every child figures out his own way to read according to how his brain works. Some ways are incredibly difficult. One teacher said that she had a little girl who struggled desperately with reading until they somehow discovered that she was trying to read the white space around the black letters instead of the letters themselves.

Repeatedly, teachers were telling me that Talmadge was given an assignment, but it was not being turned in the next day. Digging into the possibilities of why he was doing this, I found that he was extremely right-brained, creative, wise, first to notice angles in buildings and new colors on autumn leaves, and he often honestly had not heard the assignment. Like a detective, I started putting what I'd read with what teachers and Talmadge were telling me. By watching and listening to Tal, I knew that he was extremely right-brained and extremely distractable. With thirty-eight kids in his classroom, he literally could not hear the assignment if there were any distractions at the moment the teacher announced it. He was trying so hard to hear and keep up and cope with the distractions that it was giving him a headache. He was also struggling to figure out his own way to read.

To make a long story short, and a sad story happy, I began going to the classroom every day after school to get assignments and then helping him fulfill them. There were nights when I lay awake wondering where all this would end. How long could I hang on with this as my first priority with all the other demands on my time? And how would he get through college without me there to read with him?

When Tal was in ninth grade, we moved to the Washington, D.C, area, where he was put in a mainstream World History/English class in the Fairfax County schools. They ranked second in the nation for academic excellence. His reading requirement for the class—among other things—was James Michener's *The Source*. Somehow his left brain had learned to read—but not stuff like that yet. Tal and I agreed that he'd read what he could on each chapter, and then I'd finish it and have him write an outline of the rest. I found myself reading in airplanes and calling him from a hotel room to tell him what had happened. I learned so much! Though never convenient, it was actually fun! We were happy about C's and overjoyed with B's.

Somehow that year, Tal put together a lot of things and his sleeping left brain started to catch up with the wit and wisdom of his right. The last semester, when we moved back home where classes were a bit easier and I was totally occupied with another child who needed to be first priority, Talmadge got straight A's—totally on his own—and made the honor roll. It was cause for wild celebration.

Although "the world" tells us that grades are everything, in perspective, I realize that they're nice for the child's self-esteem and a parent's peace of mind, but if I had to choose between ability in academic excellence and ability to see beauty and have good old common sense, I'd choose the latter. I acknowledge that I have learned a lot more from Talmadge than he has learned from me.

Now a strapping six feet four member of the sophomore basketball team and a sixteen-year-old, with his new driver's license, thinking a lot about girls and dating, being constantly asked to turn down his new CD/stereo player, Talmadge is still a delight. He delights us not only with great academic strides but with his great wisdom. In the middle of a heated discussion recently over whether or not one of the children should go somewhere, Talmadge put his hand on my arm and said, "Mother, your decibels are too high."

A few days later, Richard really wanted me to go to a late movie with him on a school night. I, on the other hand, had been planning a reunion with six of my best high school friends whom I hadn't seen in years. They were arriving the next morning and I was totally preoccupied with thoughts of food and cleaning. But at dinnertime Richard announced to all the children that he wanted to take me "on a date." "Your mother needs to get away from everything for a while." (In actual fact, I think that *he* was the one with the proclaimed need to get away.) At 9:25 P.M., still feeling torn about where I should be, Richard urged with a little irritation, "Come on. Now we're going to be late," as he dashed out the door. "Well, it's December," I shouted sarcastically, with a little more irritation. "If you could just give me a minute to get my coat, it would be nice!"

Talmadge, who had passed me in the hall just as I said that, backed up and calmly put his arm around me. I looked up to see a tussle of curly blond hair and a twinkle in his eye. "Now, Mom," he advised, "is that the way you would talk to somebody who was taking you out on a date?"

The tension broke and I couldn't suppress a giggle.

"Touché, Talmadge!" I acknowledged, though I don't think he knew what it meant. "There you go, teaching me again!" He knew what that meant!

Last night, Talmadge came into the kitchen at about midnight and asked me what he could do to help so I could go to bed. Nobody had ever asked me that particular question. "What an amazing child," I thought.

Many "learning disabilities" are really learning advantages. Because these children with alternate learning styles do not fit the mold, we begin to think they are the ones who are disadvantaged. In actuality, the enormity of Talmadge's right brain—which sees beauty and feels compassion—just didn't leave much room for his calculative left brain. Yet somehow he has learned to compensate. The longer I live with Talmadge, the more I come to believe that I in actual fact am the one who is disadvantaged. "Learning disabilities" can be a great gift!

Surprise Thirteen
Some Days It's Hard to Tell
if You're a Mother or a Martyr

More than just a noble profession, motherhood is in reality a magnificent cause. Helping children to be happy, responsible, caring individuals, who in their own right make valuable contributions to society, can be life's most important career. There is hardly a mother alive, however, who hasn't at some point wondered whether she is a mother or a martyr. The definition of a martyr is one who endures great suffering for a belief or cause. And there is some actual suffering in motherhood, although usually the cause for feeling downtrodden is just frustration after frustration and constantly feeling that you have more on your plate than you can possibly do—with no help in sight.

I learned a long time ago that the best way to deal with wild frustrations is to write them down, then confront them and examine them. It's much easier to write in a journal when things are rosy or a wonderful event has happened that you want to remember. But it's probably far more important to write incidents down when things aren't going so well. We could all share examples of times when we were experiencing the Martyr Syndrome. Rich or poor, self-confident or timid, every mother is bound to have similar martyrlike days. Here are a couple of mine. The first two were written in my journal when our children were small, and the third when our oldest child had left for college.

Lately I'm feeling as though everyone else in our family comes first! I can't sleep because the baby cries or one of the little boys wets and I have to change the boy and the bed. I can't eat because every time I open my mouth to put food in, someone needs a note for school, breaks a two-quart jug full of milk, wants a private consultation, or I get a call from the PTA.

The other morning I was determined to get to an aerobics class. It seemed that every time I had tried for a month to get there, something had always come up so that I couldn't. As I determinedly got ready, vowing that this was the morning I was going to take care of myself first, no matter what, two cute preschool friends popped in for a visit.

"Good, they can keep my little boys occupied while I get ready," I thought. No sooner had they settled down to play than one of them came with a plea for help to unsnap his pants so that he could go to the bathroom. I hurriedly obliged and told him to use the upstairs bathroom because the downstairs bathroom sink was plugged. (Seven-year-old Josh, who lives in another world most of the time, hadn't noticed as he brushed his teeth that morning—and there was water all over the downstairs bathroom floor.)

I was trying to throw the dishes in the dishwasher before I left when I heard a scream from the bathroom: "Mrs. Eyre, Mrs. Eyre, the toilet's running over."

Instantly furious—not at the child, but at the toilet—I dashed in the bathroom and started madly mopping up the water with every towel I could get my hands on. I had, the day before, paid a plumber $70 to fix that toilet, which had run over so many times that it had ruined the ceiling in the bathroom below, which I had just paid a carpenter and painter a fortune to replace.

I was making some progress with the water when the other four-year-old came running up the stairs, screaming, "They're spilling the beans! They're spilling the beans!" Totally miffed, I stomped off to the food storage room, where I stood in the doorway aghast. There before my very eyes were two three-year-olds, squealing and giggling with delight, and they were playing what looked like "Singing in the Rain," with 50 pounds of unpopped popcorn! Little yellow kernels were flying like thousands of hard yellow raindrops falling from the sky in a spring shower.

"STOP!" I shouted, as both boys, caught in the act, jumped like kernels of hot corn popping themselves. There was dead silence as we all viewed the dastardly deed.

The whole series of events was unbelievably preposterous! Needless to say, I never made it to my aerobics class. Another thing I needed to do for me was not going to get done.

Even as I write, I have stopped to change a diaper, retrieved the baby out of the china closet, found a pen for a six-year-old, answered the phone twice, solved three cases of sibling rivalry, admired Noah's "tree" which he had been "writing," answered the door, picked the baby up out of a puddle of milk on the kitchen table, and dragged two busy boys out of Daddy's den twice so he could write.

The next entry was written a few months later, just after the birth of our last child:

Charity is four months old, and I'm feeling the Martyr Syndrome and that Fat Syndrome all at once. I'm definitely feeling like I'm not in charge. I can't exercise very well because of my back and ankle, still painful from the car accident this summer. I can't quit eating because I'm nursing the baby. I've been patient with being caught between a rock and a hard place until now. But I think I must just have hit the saturation point!

Years later, I wrote:

It is Monday. The day began with squeals of delight. It was the first snowstorm after a long drought. By the time the kids were ready to leave for school, the front hall was strewn with soggy snow pants, snow-caked boots, and mismatched mittens.

My noble plans to get all the children completely finished with their music practice and jobs by the time they left for school were dashed. By 8:15, no practicing had been done, and breakfast had not crossed anyone's mind. They were saturated with the exhilaration of the first snow. Amidst shrieks of laughter as the children spewed out stories of their snowballs and snowmen, I sent them off to school and then did all their jobs, made dinner in the crockpot, tried to clear a path to get in the front door, dragged down a batch of washing, sighed deeply at the sight of batches of washing done but not folded and some folded but not put away, and mounds of ironing and leftovers from teenagers' sewing projects.

I closed the door, tried to forget it, and attempted to make Charity and myself presentable enough to appear at an aerobics class. After dashing to the bank to make a deposit lest I become overdrawn . . . again . . . and a quick stop at the video store to drop off the weekend video before they opened, so I wouldn't have to pay a late fee, I arrived at exercise class twenty-five minutes late and "enjoyed" thirty-five minutes of pain and suffering as I tried to "put myself first."

Next, on my way to run errands with two preschoolers, I realized that I was the car pool for the afternoon kindergartners. I turned the car around, picked them up, and, after driving through for fast food, I rushed to the mall to get a Cub Scout shirt and a new coat for Eli, who had, in the tradition of his siblings, lost his at school.

During the process of these purchases, two-year-old Charity got lost three times, and I suffered through four kicking and screaming tantrums because she couldn't have what she wanted. Eli, our toothless, freckled five-year-old, became a "basket case" because we couldn't stop at the candy machines.

Just as I was dashing off to pick up the elementary school kids, I saw an old friend who introduced me to a married daughter and told her what darling children I had. "Thanks," I said, glad that she didn't know the whole truth. "I needed that!"

Next it was on to a promised "mommy date" with Talmadge, which was a reward for wearing his headgear more than any of his siblings for the past week (four children were wearing orthodontic paraphernalia). We headed for the frozen yogurt store, which was my idea of a fun mommy date. I soon learned that he had his heart set on his idea of a fun mommy date, which was to go to the model store to get a new chassis for his remote-control car. By the time we got home, it was too late to eat the stew I had prepared before we had to leave for Dad's basketball game. We all went for a family-gym evening and I tried to watch the game, but was interrupted every two minutes by a child either begging for 50 cents for the soft-drink machine or needing to go to the bathroom.

While Richard had fun taking the other kids to get frozen yogurt after the game, Saydi and I hurried off to her cello lesson. I listened with my ears and balanced my checkbook with my eyes, feeling guilty because I had forgotten to bring a piece of paper so I could write a letter to our college daughter.

Upon our arrival at home, that daughter was on the phone, calling from Wellesley. When she talked to me, she told me that her contact lenses were tearing at her eyes, the water was turning her hair green, and that she couldn't find a date for the formal dinner dance. When she talked to Richard, she told him what a wonderful time she'd been having and how beautiful the campus was.

The call was the end of a perfect day for one who started out thinking of herself as a bit of a martyr. I was too tired to tackle the laundry room or sew on the Scout badges as I had planned. I found myself kicking boots down the hall and muttering about how much I hated winter. By then it was 11:00 P.M., and I found Charity—who had gotten out of bed because she wasn't a bit tired because she had sneaked a nap in the car—walking around in the hall, having taken off her pajamas and put her clothes back on, complete with shoes and socks, concluding her eighteen-hour symphony of tears because she was hungry.

Not at all nicely, I put her back in bed and dropped into my own. Completely depressed and miserable, I realized that my mood was somewhat due to PMS, yet another trial to suffer! Just then Richard came in and said, "I forgot to tell you that they need two articles from you for the newsletter tomorrow morning!"

"Why can he never tell me things like that a little more than twelve hours in advance!" I fumed. Feeling like a total, unadulterated martyr, I counted to ten. It didn't make me feel any better. Just before I put the covers over my head, I said, "I can't do it . . . and you . . . are stupid."

Not very profound words from a martyr about to die. Even though Richard had no idea where I was coming from, somehow it made me feel better.

All martyr days do not have a happy ending, but this one did. The

next morning Richard handed me a handwritten poem at 6:30 A.M. that
pointed out the things he appreciated about me. How divine—to realize
that somebody actually appreciated the efforts of the martyr . . . before
her death!

I walked directly to the bathroom, locked the door, let the kids make
their own breakfast, and wrote this entry to the tune of a two-year-old
who could smell me like a dog, beating on the door.

Incidents like these are part of what I call the mother's Martyr Syndrome. If we are not careful, we can convince ourselves that life is only a series of unappreciated sacrifices, tribulations, vexations, adversities, ordeals, annoyances, and plagues—usually suffered for a good cause! We can so easily become depressed and "witchy," and begin to think our life unbearable and insufferable, unless we can keep the following points in mind:

1. On some days when involved in "mundania," a certain amount of martyrdom is inevitable; it comes with the job, and in the case of PMS, with the gender.

2. Martyrdom can actually be good for you. Think of it as a way to offer anonymous service and to develop charity. It is a good way to enhance compassion and magnify empathy for the needs of others, too.

3. Part of the Martyr Syndrome is brought on by ourselves and our inability to get others to help. Doing things for our husband and children when they are perfectly capable of doing them themselves does not do them a favor. It is actually a disservice. When you're feeling overwhelmed, tell your husband and children and outline some ways that they can help. Don't suffer silently—put your foot down and demand some relief! Stop punishing your family by saying, "Never mind, I'll do it myself." Make them help when they can, even though it's often easier to do it yourself.

4. If you are living with a husband, enlist his help to get the children to be more dutiful and helpful. Somehow putting him in charge of seeing that some things get done makes him more helpful as well.

5. When a series of wild events occur and you feel fully qualified to be a martyr, the overall effect is usually hysterical. Learn to laugh! Sometimes the humor takes a little time to settle in, but other times it can be immediate. (The popcorn scene was funny almost immediately. We all ended up laughing uncontrollably.) I like what Sebastien Nicholas Chamfort said, "The most completely lost of all days is the one on which we have not laughed."

6. Write things down the next time you experience the Martyr Syndrome. It's good therapy and helps you realize that the cause is still noble. And martyr or not, you are going to live. Or, as Agatha Christie said, "I like living. I have sometimes been wildly, despairingly, acutely miserable, racked with sorrow, but through it all I still know quite certainly just to be alive is a grand thing."

Surprise Fourteen
There Is Speed in Going Slow

What I thought was one of my greatest attributes has turned out to be one of my greatest faults, that is, my need to be on time. For years, despite my exhaustive efforts to herd everyone out the door early, I always ended up in a race to the car, screaming, "Hurry, hurry, we're late!" Inevitably somebody lost his shoes, sat in the mud, had to go to the bathroom, or forgot something critical just as we were dashing out the door.

One Mother's Day, the kids give me a hand-drawn poster with caricatures of each member of the family. Over each head was a little balloon which contained each person's most common saying at that time. In my case, they simply could not limit themselves to one saying. There were four: "Where are your shoes?" "Where is my purse?" "Practice!" and "Get in the car—we're late!"

"What about me really bothers you most?" I asked our two oldest girls. It didn't take either of them very long to answer. "Mom," they said sheepishly at first, and then with more and more confidence, "when we're late for something, you can't get over it! You keep raving on about how late we are and how much we needed to be on time, but by then we're already late and we can't do a thing about it. We can't turn back the clocks. If you could just quit worrying about it and get us there, it would really be terrific!"

Observing myself during the next few weeks, I realized that they were exactly right. It was an obsession with me to be on time. Especially to church. Over and over again on Sunday I was saying things like, "Are you ready? Get your little brother ready. What are you doing in the bathroom so long? What are you going to do with your hair? How could you sleep so long? You always think there's more time than there is." By the time I got out the door, even after all the yelling, we were still late.

"Why didn't you hurry a little faster? I told you to get the diaper bag ready early this morning. You should always find your shoes on Saturday night!" I would rave on.

One Sunday I got smart. "We are walking out this door at 9:30 A.M.," I announced as soon as everyone was up. "If you're ready, you can ride. If you're not, you'll have to walk. I suggest that you get ready by nine-fifteen, but it's up to you. I'm not going to say any more about it." And then I added, ironically, "Let's hurry so we don't have to rush!" They knew what I meant.

I stayed calm and proceeded to get myself ready and to help the little ones. Of the nine child-bodies at our house, three needed a little prodding, and six needed help with hair. I held a firm grip on my temper and at the appointed hour pleasantly told the two "fatalities" to hold hands and walk down the hill to the church. Amazingly, the next Sunday everyone was ready on time.

As much as I hate to admit it, I was one of the major problems in getting anywhere on time. As soon as I realized this, I decided to change my approach. I began to discover "the speed of going slow." Whenever I was late, instead of being frantic, ruffling feathers, and making everybody feel uptight, I tried to become more deliberate. I moved steadily but was consciously slowing down my mind while being more aware of each movement. Somehow things seemed to happen easier, and better, and incredibly, I got to more appointments on time.

I am beginning to see that my rushing to prepare meals, to get kids to lessons on time, and being a little nasty on the way is never really worth it. I realized that being on time is often at the expense of a relationship, and that is never right. When I hurry, I often break things, damage cars, and hurt feelings. I still feel the need to be on time, and try as I might, I often can't help raising everybody's blood pressure in the process. But I realize how much more quickly I can actually get things done if I remain calm and collected.

Another thing hurrying does is prevent you from seeing what's really important. After a parenting conference once, a young mother explained her rebellious feelings as she was hurrying to prepare a quick meal. Arriving home late after work, she was greeted by a crying baby, starving children, and a husband who was supposed to be taking care of everything.

She related, "I was just feeling so 'used' as I struggled alone in the kitchen to meet everybody's needs. Then my husband called me from the front yard."

"Hey, Karen, come out and watch this beautiful storm coming in," he yelled.

That made her even madder. She said to herself, "Why do I always have to be the one with my nose to the grindstone? I don't have time to watch a storm come in. And he wouldn't ask if he knew about the storm that is going on in my head!"

But she stopped herself short and remembered that her relationship with her husband and her love for nature were much more important than having dinner on time. She felt her inner storm recede as that beautiful storm outside rolled in.

Often our desire to be on time can have a negative effect on a relationship with a child, a husband, or a friend. Obviously we want to be on time for the doctor appointment or the music lesson. Nor can we let our children be perpetually late for school. But the next time you feel hassled and pressured because you're late for something, think for a moment about how important it really is to be on time. If it isn't crucial, relax and enjoy the moment.

If it is, consciously slow your mind down. Say to yourself, "I can get this done faster if I remain calm." Be doubly aware of what is happening. Consciously try to slow things down in your mind while you move your body toward the goal. Put on seat belts and be more aware of traffic and calm ways to maneuver your way through it without panicking. Somehow you will get there faster and get more done when you are consciously aware of being articulate and careful about getting to a place on time. You'll be amazed at "the speed of going slow."

Actually, Richard taught me this concept. He is so good at it that he even claims he can slow time down. Although I don't know how he does it, he often gets us to speaking engagements in less time than it takes to get there—without breaking the speed limit. It's incredible!

If you are a high-stress, type A personality, you may find an unexpected friend in time. Discover the speed of going slow.

Surprise Fifteen
The Kid Is Always Right
(from His/Her Perspective)

Hot tears streamed down my face. My eyes were red and puffy, and my face felt as though if someone were to touch it with a pin, it would explode like a balloon. "I'm going to remember how this feels, and someday I'm going to write a book about parents' injustices to children!" I thought at twelve, with childish logic. I had just been denied the privilege of going somewhere I felt I desperately needed to go with my friends. Wherever it was, it seemed extremely important to my social wellness. I was sure that my life would never be the same. At that moment, I was sure that my mother was related to witch Cruella in *One Hundred and One Dalmatians,* which I had just seen for the first time. For the life of me, I can't remember where I wanted to go or why it was so important. I can only recall saying to myself, "Now *remember* this great injustice, Linda! Someday you are going to write a book about the world as seen through the eyes of a helpless, hopeless child who has absolutely no control over her own life."

Putting things in context, I have a wonderful, amazing mother who probably was just having a bad day with hormones. She was almost always fair, even though she insisted that I not go anywhere until my practicing and work were done. Time passed, and I not only forgot my pledge, I became a wicked witch myself. I know there are times when my children now often feel cruelly misunderstood.

Through the years, I have grown attached to the word "remember." "Remember, remember," is an important admonition often repeated in Scripture. Remembering is part of transposing those utterly human feelings of needing to be understood, from childhood to motherhood. Although I haven't done that book yet, this chapter is an attempt to fulfill that dream.

Years ago I attended a seminar entitled "Executive Excellence." About two thousand business executives in attendance were learning to improve their business skills, particularly in the area of management. Having decided that no one there could have a more difficult management job than I did, I went, not as a business executive, but as a mother. I was pleased and amused to find that almost everything that was said applied perfectly to my career as a mother.

Tom Peters, one of the speakers, and the author of *In Pursuit of Excellence*, was asked, "What about the old adage: 'The customer is always right'? What do you do when the customer is wrong?" His snappy answer was a surprise to many in the audience. "The customer is *never* wrong! Neither party is right nor wrong. You have to try to look at the problem through the other person's eyes. You will find that by looking at the problem from his perspective, although it may not be correct from your perspective, you can see why he thinks he is right.

"It's often hard to take," he admitted, "but a great manager can always say: 'I see your point. I understand what you mean. You're right. Let's work this out.'"

Richard and I have long been fans of our friend Stephen Covey, who was also there that day, advocating a win/win mentality. The belief that both parties with conflicting ideas can learn to understand the other's viewpoint and progress to a resolution in which both parties win, has its greatest application in the home. Too often, we become authoritarian parents who think we are always right. When it comes to a conflict, we don't bother to extend our own children the same courtesy we would to a brother or a friend. If the child disagrees, he/she is always wrong. Right?

Just after school started this year, our eight-year-old son came to me dejected and forlorn, complaining that life was too hard for him. "I'm supposed to practice the piano every day," he wailed, "and make my bed and clean my room and sweep the floor after breakfast and dinner. I can't keep this up. It's just too much!"

I giggled inwardly but tried not to let my inner smile over his misery show too much on the outside. "Jonah, that's not too much," I began. "If you hurry, you can get all that done in a very short time and have the rest of the time for yourself."

But he had quit listening after the first sentence and was raving on about all the trials of his life, his hard work at school, his terrible Saturday chores, and especially this new added burden of practicing the piano each day.

I was beginning to feel a little annoyed when suddenly something he said pushed a button in my memory. I remembered clearly one Saturday morning when my mother called me to get up and start my Saturday chores.

I remembered being bitterly disappointed that I was now old enough to help with the work and was beginning to be an older child. I reluctantly realized that my carefree days of babyhood and early childhood were over, and that I might never get to sleep in on a Saturday morning again for the rest of my life! I had not thought of that agonizing moment since it happened, but remembering it then made me much more sympathetic to Jonah's dilemma.

Suddenly I could see that what he was saying was absolutely true from his perspective. I was glad that I hadn't had a chance to express my worst thoughts, which were: "Jonah, that is absolutely ridiculous! Compared to what I have to do every day, your plight is so tiny that it is not even worth mentioning! So many of your hours are wasted. It's so important to begin to learn responsibility. You're big enough to bite the bullet on these things."

Instead, I said, "Jonah, I know just how you feel." And I told him about my childhood experience. He smiled a little, and then I said, "Now, you really are working lots harder this year. Let's see what we can do to make things easier for you."

His heavy responsibilities really didn't change much, but he agreed that he thought maybe he could handle things by the end of our conversation. The most important point to him was that he knew I thought he was right. Much of his burden was lifted by sympathy and understanding.

One afternoon when the little children arrived home from school, an older child, anxious to celebrate because she had no homework, wanted to ride her bike with a friend down to a nearby shopping center. All it took was one child to mention the possibility, and there was a chorus of "Can I go, too?" One other child was already in the front yard with his friend, both on their bikes, so I said, "Okay, Shawni and Jonah, you take your friends and go, and you other two stay home and baby-sit while I go take care of a neighbor. You two can go next time."

With hot, angry tears streaming down his face, Joshua complained of this injustice as I flew out the door to help someone. I didn't have time for perspective or sympathy or understanding. When I got home, Joshua's face was swollen and red from crying. I found that before asking to go, he had worked hard to finish his homework because he had big assignments coming up the rest of the week and that had been the only afternoon he could play with a friend.

I apologized for not having time to listen and tried to help him see things from my perspective. He tried to understand, but the fact remained that I had prioritized helping a neighbor—which really could have been done later—over his desperate (from his perspective) need to relax and be with a friend.

Such is life! Yet, I keep thinking that if I can just remember more often that "the kid is always right" (from his/her perspective), I can do a lot to settle conflicts in the home peacefully.

"Easier said than done" applies well here, but one conflict settled with sympathy and understanding out of every ten conflicts that occur is better than none. One of the great unexpected treasures that I gained from all that piano and violin practicing as a child was not "practice makes perfect," but that practicing makes you better. Practice looking at the world through your child's eyes. And practice remembering. It's great exercise!

Surprise Sixteen
Adversity Is Actually Good for You; or, if Life Is Just a Bowl of Cherries, Hire a Wolf to Knock at Your Door

I remember the summer when *Jurassic Park* hit the movie theaters. At our house, we had been fascinated by the wild scientific possibilities that the book proposed. For several weeks before the movie was released, the older children and Richard and I had been reading the book in order to be better informed when we saw the movie. So that we could all read it together, we bought two paperbacks and actually tore them apart so that we could each be reading a section at a time. Eventually, it got hard to keep track of who had the next section. Dissected parts of *Jurassic Park* lay all over the house. When the night came to go to the movie, we realized how much we had been talking about it when our seven-year-old, who thought she was going to be left behind, pleaded, "I want to go to *Drastic Park* too!" We giggled, thinking it would be a better name anyway.

Many days I feel as though our house is actually "Drastic Park"! One day when we called home to see how the children were doing while we were on a three-day book tour, we could hear someone screaming in the background. Talmadge assured us that everything was going to be all right. It was just that Noah had gotten a toenail stuck in his eye (a household hazard I hadn't thought of). Also that they were trying to think of how to get the eighteen-month-old out of the bathroom because she had gone in, locked the door, then gotten lipstick out of the drawer and made her hands so greasy she couldn't turn the knob to get out. I still remember him saying, "Don't worry, Mom, we'll work it out. Everything is going to be just fine!"

Drastic Park at our home comes complete with dinosaurs in the form of the daily disasters that abide there. I have children who at the moment remind me of the spitters and raptors; occasionally, a big "Rex" stomps in!

I talked to a friend the other day who felt she was living in her own "Drastic Park" for the past ten years. She and I had known each other since college; she was one of the most dependable, cheerful, capable people I knew. About ten years ago, her husband left her, and she went back to teaching to support her four growing children. Each day was a struggle financially, physically, and emotionally . . . just to survive.

Three years ago she found a man with five wonderful children whose wife had died, and she was persuaded to marry him. A blended family was a challenge, but things really started getting hairy when, after a few months of marriage, her husband lost his job, went into a deep depression, and became incapable of functioning normally. Now she had nine children and an incapacitated husband, all depending on her care.

At Christmastime after a short period of feeling sorry for herself, my friend decided to pull herself out of her self-pity and do something for someone else. With a plateful of goodies on her way to a young widow's home, she slipped on the ice and broke her foot in several places, necessitating a steel plate in her foot and three months in bed. Pretty drastic.

Yet, in telling me all this, she couldn't say enough about all the things she had learned about herself, her children, and other people's children through the wide variety of trials she had undergone. Armed with a good dose of the drastic realities of life, she was ready to write a book to help others who were going through similar trials.

Just this week, I heard a magnificent talk by a vibrant older friend who was going far away from home on a mission for our church with his wife. This man was one of the best tennis doubles players in the city, which is a surprise only when you realize that one of his legs is considerably shorter than the other as a result of an accident he had as a nine-year-old. A terrible infection followed, and the sure knowledge that he would never be able to participate in contact sports again. As he described his devastation on being told that he would be physically handicapped for the rest of his days, we felt sad that his life had been changed forever. Yet, at the end of his talk, he said without reservation that he had learned so much love and compassion, and had gained so many friends through his trials, that if he had his life to live over, he would wish for that same accident.

I love the following quotes: "We could never learn to be brave and patient if there were only joy in the world" (Helen Keller) . . . "To live is so startling, that there is little time for anything else" (Emily Dickinson) . . . and "It is better to light a candle than to curse the darkness" (Eleanor Roosevelt).

Continually I am amazed at the unending array of lessons that can be learned from life's adversities. Often I hear people say that they wouldn't ask for their trials, given a choice, but they wouldn't give up the valuable things they have learned from them, either. Our children all go on eighteen-month to two-year missions for our church between the ages of nineteen and twenty-one. They perform humanitarian service and essentially forget themselves as they give help to others. Having had the first three move off and return to us (one to Bulgaria, one to Romania, and one to England), I think I can safely say that it would have been very hard for them to leave if they had known how difficult the day-to-day struggles would be, but they unequivocally would have to say there is no way we could have kept them home if they could have known the joy these experiences would bring to their lives.

I believe in adversity so much as a teaching tool that I have hung a little saying on the walls of my mind from some anonymous someone who had obviously learned the value of adversity: "If life is just a bowl of cherries, hire a wolf to knock at your door." My friends look at me like I'm crazy when I quote that in my attempt to explain why we often move back and forth between two homes—one in the Rocky Mountains and one in suburban Washington, D.C. We are lucky enough to be able to come back to the same home base, after moving the children around. Moving has been one of their greatest trials and also one of their great blessings.

After a month of sitting in the lunchroom alone at a new high school in Virginia where we had moved for the year, Jonah, our sixteen-year-old, came home one day and said, "I'll tell you one thing. When I get home, I'm not going to just sit and laugh with my friends at lunch, I'm going to look around and find some new kid who looks like they need a friend, and go talk to him." And he has. All of our children are very sensitive to the needs of new kids who come into their schools and new faces at parties, because they know how it feels to be insecure, lonely, and apprehensive about new situations.

I saw a videotape by Gary Smalley, a terrific "relationship" therapist, recently in which he used an analogy which was intended to apply to everyone, but which is especially meaningful to mothers. He was talking about the need we all feel to have someone fix the problems in our lives . . . to light our light bulbs, so to speak. His point was that the only one who, in the end, can get us through the adversity in our lives is ourselves. We can't wait for our husbands and children, our mothers or our friends, to make us happy. Ultimately, we have to know that the only way to survive adversity is to rely on ourselves; and I would like to add in my case, to "cast your burdens on the Lord."

A perfect analogy for this, as he pointed out, is an oyster. The outside of an oyster is sometimes pretty crusty-looking, having weathered the rigors of the sea, but inside sometimes is found a beautiful pearl, which has been formed there by a little irritating grain of sand. Sometimes, the bigger the grain of sand or the more grains of sand, the more beautiful and lustrous the pearl.

In our own lives, we find our own pearl which has formed in our souls because of the difficulties we have endured and the lessons we have learned from small or great irritations. It is truly a pearl of great price . . . more valuable than any worldly possession. It makes us who we are, and cultivates our compassion and love for others who may be in the same difficult position. It stretches our ability to cope with life and its problems, and expands our understanding of what is really happening in what seems an impossible situation.

Those who have endured such terrible things as physical or sexual abuse or the death of a close friend or relative can look at such major life-changing experiences in two ways: as destructive, cancerous, and shattering, or as experiences that have made them stronger, more sympathetic, understanding, and compassionate, and much better able to aid others who may need relief in similar situations. Of course, those kind of experiences we wouldn't ask for. But there is no way to replicate the luster that they bring to "the pearl" of one's soul if they are used wisely to help others cope with similar experiences in years to come.

If your "Drastic Park" seems too heavy to bear right now, just think of the pearl that is forming. It may take some time to be ready to open the crusty shell and expose the beautiful jewel that is taking shape, but just know that when you behold what that "grain of sand" has done, and how well you can use it to help others, you may be more grateful than you can now imagine. It was Virgil who said: "Perhaps, someday, even this distress will be a joy to recall."

On the other hand, if life is just a bowl of cherries, and you need to start working on that pearl, hire a wolf to knock at your door!

Surprise Seventeen
The Only Thing That's Always the Same
Is That Every Child Is Different

The age-old question whether we gain our personalities through environment or heredity will probably never be fully resolved. My theory supposes "a little of each and a lot of neither."

One morning in the middle of my ninth pregnancy, with the help of an ultrasound scan, I watched a miracle: A tiny new little individual, who sprang into earthly existence only twenty-one weeks before, moved suspended in her watery, weightless world, moving arms and legs freely. Hooked to an umbilical lifeline like an astronaut in space, we saw her face—her eyes, nose, and lips—like a black and white negative. She was totally unaware that we were watching, of course. It gave me chills to realize once again that somebody was in there. I am convinced that this new little girl was already an individual—as unique and different from her brothers and sisters as they are from each other.

All nine of our children "on the outside world" were as different as the colors in the rainbow, all beautiful and complementary to each other. Just when we think we have found the solution for one child's problems, the next one comes along with the same problem but a nature that needs to be handled in a totally different way—or with totally different problems and needs.

This uniqueness manifests itself every day at our house. All the children work within the same boundaries, called "family laws." They all have jobs to do; they all accept responsibility—but in their own ways.

Two get up exactly when their alarms ring and are practicing right on time. One of those two is angry most of the morning; the other is seldom ruffled by anything. Two others have to be literally dragged from their beds. One gets right to work as soon as she realizes she's awake; the other manages to pass the next two and a half hours doing absolutely nothing unless someone stands over him every waking moment.

Some are gifted in music. One started out being the worst violinist in the orchestra, but progressed, slowly but surely, until she became first chair. Another almost effortlessly absorbs music, but won't practice no matter what the bribe. A third couldn't play well if his life depended on it (for this year, anyway).

Some of our preschoolers have been curious about letters and shapes and colors; others couldn't see them even when they were pointed out. Very quiet ones listen for hours to those who cannot stop talking. Some get wonderful grades. One worries about grades incessantly—and unnecessarily—while another usually never worries when he should.

While some are rich with the money they have earned, others are penniless—even though both are presented with the same opportunities to earn money. The list could go on forever, and I'm sure that similar differences between children apply in your house.

While this uniqueness is one of the most wonderful things to behold in our homes, it is also the thing that can turn us into instant witches, especially when we realize that we have our own uniqueness to cope with, too—as well as our husband's.

How do we walk the tightrope of uniqueness? How do we balance our own uniqueness with the uniqueness of husband and children? Let's go back to music for a minute. How hard do we push children to practice? Do we push them whether they seem talented or not because it is a good discipline or because they may bloom later? Do they practice every day, or only when we force them; only when we reward them, or only when they want to?

I have a friend who wants her children to be responsible and to be great musicians. (Incidentally, they are!) She calls practicing "milking the cows." The cows must be milked morning and night, day after day, month after month, year after year. Other mothers produce talented children by letting them practice when they want to—because they love it. (Not many children qualify for this type of music education, I might add.) Some mothers push so hard that the children never touch their instruments again after they leave home. Some grown children scold their parents endlessly for not making them practice when they were too young to know what they wanted or needed.

I am sorry to say that I am not going to give answers or solutions for these complex matters. The answers lie with you, and they depend on how much thought you give to the uniqueness of your children. Even after all that, we probably still make mistakes.

We do need to keep two things in mind, however, as we analyze, sympathize, and tyrannize:

1. If our children do not keep pace with us—with our wants and desires for them, our needs and expectations—it may be because they "hear their own drummer." We need to allow them to develop in their own way, no matter how much we may want them to develop in *our* way. We still have to provide them with parameters for their own security, but children must have room to be individuals.

Maybe the "other world" they are in is actually better than ours! We can learn a great deal from them if we will listen to them, instead of insisting that they always do it our way.

2. Contrary to what we may have heard, children are not like clay—which we can mold into whatever we want if we try hard enough. They are seedlings. The seed of what they are has already been planted from the moment they began their existence. Some may be orange trees and other might be lemons. It is our job, as the gardeners, to observe, water, expose to the sun, weed, provide fertilizer, and nurture, in order to make the most beautiful plant possible from the seedlings we are given.

At an International University in Australia, sponsored by the Young Presidents' Organization, we found ourselves on the faculty with a fascinating professor from Harvard who had done extensive work with twins. His life's work was spent analyzing the behavior of twins, to the point of reuniting twins who had been separated at birth and adopted and raised by different families. He loved seeking these people out and reuniting them with their siblings. His stories were fascinating as he told of standing them against a wall at the airport so that he could take their picture. Often their very stance—whether it was folding their arms or crossing their ankles—was precisely the same. Stories abounded of these twins having precisely the same interests, of naming the dogs the same name, and of mispronouncing the same words. Even though their environments were very different, he had concluded that their genes were amazingly influential.

While he was passing on this information in one room, Richard and I were teaching the principle of the seedlings in the next. Over lunch, we had a chance to compare notes. "Does this mean that you believe we are totally products of our genes, then?" we asked. "Good grief, no," he said. "I have a son I tried to make into a scientist for fifteen years. Finally I decided to give up and let him do what he really wanted to do. He just graduated from the finest art academy in America with honors." We explained our seedling analogy and he loved it. "It's all a matter of watching kids to see what they really love and what they excel at," Richard said, "and then being smart enough to give them the encouragement and training to excel." The professor agreed.

With nine children, we have found no two to be even remotely alike. We've discovered this to be a great blessing when parents we speak with begin to explain their child's strange characteristics. No matter what the problem, we're almost always able to light up as they describe "symptoms," and say, "We have one just like that! Let us tell you what we tried. . . ."

The greatest gift a parent can have is to be a good watcher. As we watch our children to discover their uniqueness, it becomes more and more apparent what they need for "fertilizer." Trying to make our children over into ourselves or what we wish we could have been is one of the greatest problems of parenthood. Instead of being upset by their uniqueness, celebrate it . . . and start watering!

Surprise Eighteen
A Sense of Humor Is
Your Most Important Baggage
(A Look at the Eyres' Funniest Home Videos)

As a mother, without a sense of humor . . . you're dead! I know because I have been almost dead several times. We all know that crisis plus time equals humor. Some crises take more time than others to conjure humor. The older I get, the funnier each crisis seems—sooner. Some of the following incidents, recorded on paper, sometimes years apart, would make great clips for "The Eyres' Funniest Home Videos." I know certain ones will remind you of things that have happened in your own house. Again, thinking back over your own "Funniest Home Videos," some have probably taken time to seem funny. Others will remind you of how much fun you were having. Still others will help you remember valuable lessons you learned from a very difficult situation, just as they have for me. I challenge you to write your funniest moments down for a good laugh, and for future generations to learn from as you do.

As you know from previous chapters, life at the Eyres' house is a crisis a minute. In an effort not to bore you, I am including only some of our more embarrassing ones, perhaps to make you feel better about yours.

One sunny Sunday I sat in church on a bench close to the front of the chapel, trying to cope with four children—ages five, four, two, and six months. From past experience, I knew they wouldn't just sit there quietly playing with their fingers for an hour and a half, so I had armed myself with the usual crayons, Cheerios, and writing paper. A teen-aged baby-sitter had offered to sit with me and help as Richard was (typically for that point in our marriage) out of town.

Our speaker was a prestigious church historian, who began telling wonderful "inside stories" about little-known facts in our church's history. I heard little of this as I was struggling to keep the pacifier in the baby's mouth and Cheerios in our talkative four-year-old's. After about fifteen minutes, our very strong-willed two-year-old pushed past my legs and headed straight for the podium. I froze and silently prayed that he would come back before he got to the piano. He hesitated for a moment on the steps, then headed for the speaker, where he stood by the pulpit and listened attentively for about one minute while the audience snickered. Just as I was about to retrieve him, even with my scarlet face, he headed for the piano. Before I could move but not before he played several loud notes, the baby-sitter was on her way up to get him.

Horrified, I knew he would never consent to being brought down without a struggle. I was absolutely right. Immediately he began to kick and scream as she grabbed him by the middle. Just as the poor, unsuspecting girl reached the bottom step of the podium, the two-year-old threw his arms straight in the air. Slipping through her arms, he fell kicking and screaming to the floor, directly in her path. She stumbled over him, then like a comedy of errors in slow motion, fell right on top of him.

Mortified, knowing that every eye in the audience had completely forgotten the speaker and was watching the drama in the side pew unfold, my only thought was to get this screaming mass out of the chapel. I grabbed the little guy like a sack of potatoes under my left arm, and scooped up the fussing baby in her infant seat with my right. Unfortunately, the arm of the infant seat somehow gave way and the baby did an instant double somersault. To the horror of the audience and me, she landed directly on her head on the floor!

It was the longest speed walk I can remember . . . down that aisle, with a screaming bundle under each arm, to the safety of the foyer. I quickly examined the baby's head for bruises, bumps, or cuts, and luckily there were none. Within moments, one of the elders of the church, who was sitting on the stand and also happened to be a brain surgeon, had excused himself and come to check the poor baby's head (which he assured me was okay). What an outrageous series of catastrophic errors! Although it took a good two weeks for this incident to seem funny, it now provides us one of our best family giggles.

At one point in our marriage, we moved to England for three years. We took four children with us and came back with six, having had two babies in British hospitals. One little clip I recorded in a letter at the end of our third year, when our children all had perfect British accents, reminded me of how much fun we had during those years.

Our first British-born baby, two-year-old Jonah, trotted into my bedroom one morning with a gleam of mischief in his eye while I was sitting in the rocking chair, nursing our new baby, Talmadge. Jonah had a large new open tube of toothpaste in his hand and a wicked grin on his face. Seeing that I was immobile, he ignored my pleas to hand it over. He diverted my attention and somehow got the toothpaste under the rocker of my chair. I didn't notice the ploy until it was too late.

In the meantime, four-year-old Saydi came running into the room with two big crocodile tears in her eyes and in her high, whining voice said, "Mummy, Joshie says to me to eat peppah and I don't want to eat peppah. It stings my mouth!"

Still nursing the baby, I calmed her fears about the "peppah," and then saw Jonah out of the corner of my eye, this time with a tube of purple liquid eyeshadow which someone had given me and I couldn't bring myself to throw away. I waited until he got the lid off and started to squeeze before I dashed after him, the poor baby still hanging on, and chased him around the room until I retrieved the purple guck.

I had scarcely settled back into my chair before I heard water running in the adjoining bathroom and Saydi and Jonah chattering to each other. Running water demands attention, so I interrupted the baby again and went to check. I found Jonah up to his elbows, sweater and all, in the water in the sink and Saydi drinking out of the rubber stopper from the bathtub. They were having some kind of wonderful tea party.

As I wrung out the sweater and cleaned up the blob of tooth-paste squashed on the carpet, talked Josh into coaxing the other two preschoolers off to the playroom while I finished feeding the baby, I couldn't help but smile as they trotted down the hall and out of sight. Saydi was saying, "Do you want me to tell you Cinderella's telephone numbah . . . 91238475647586–9." What fun we're having!

Back in America, but not too much longer after that, I found myself one day on the way to a certain department store to return two big bed-spreads, which I had taken home for my mother to "try," neither of which had worked. In my usual overoptimistic manner, I had decided that I would have just enough time to return them with four preschool-ers in tow, and still be able to pick up our two older children at the ele-mentary school within a half an hour.

"I'll just slip in and out unnoticed," I thought, as I piled the little quartet out of the car. I cringed a bit as I noticed that one had flimsy, unmatched flipflops on his feet, most had peanut butter on their faces left over from our hasty retreat, and three had scraggly-looking hair. "At least the baby is bald," I muttered to myself, as I hurried them in.

In the store, I discovered that there was no elevator. Since the home furnishings were on the second floor, I quickly organized a plan for the escalator. Because they would not allow open strollers on the "moving stairs," I folded ours up, hung it over my right arm, and perched the baby, happily sucking on his fist and completely unaware of my dilemma, on that same arm. In my left hand I tightly clenched the black garbage bag into which I had placed the bedspreads to protect them from the peanut butter.

In front of me was five-year-old Josh, studying the mechanics of the escalator, and two-and-a-half-year-old Jonah, fidgeting and shuffling with his thinly clad feet. Behind me was cute four-year-old Saydi in her self-chosen orphan outfit, a nice mixture of peanut butter and jam from ear to ear, obviously enjoying the ride and singing "Tomorrow" embar-rassingly loud as we moved upward, thus destroying my plan to remain inconspicuous.

As we rolled to the top, the five-year-old got off with a grand gesture of accomplishment. The two-year-old, however, bless his screeching lit-tle heart, panicked and bolted, deciding he was *not* getting off under any circumstances. The scene that resulted was hysterical. Josh started yelling, "Hey, Mom, Jonah's *stuck!*" Suddenly Jonah was yelling at the top of his lungs and all I could think of was the possibilities of those bare little toes being mangled in the "iron teeth." Saydi, who was being helplessly bashed into me from behind, was bellowing like a sick cow, and poor little baby Talmadge was screaming with horror because I had lurched to grab Jonah and pushed him onto the landing with all my might. Talmadge meanwhile had fallen backwards and was literally hanging upside down like a trapeze artist from my bended arm, which was clamped on his knees like a steel trap.

Although it was only a few seconds, it seemed as though it took an eternity to get us all off that escalator. Three of the four children were wailing. I did my best to comfort them while feeling completely disgusted with myself for trying such a stupid thing. "How could you be so dumb," I scolded myself, as though I were a naughty child. "What in the world are you doing with all these kids!"

Quickly I tried to compose myself, dry the tears, and hurry on, as I knew our grade schoolers would be waiting. As luck would have it, I got stuck behind two very slow old ladies picking through knitting yarn on a very narrow aisle. One of them had on high-topped, black rubber boots with flopping buckles, and the other had an old-fashioned pillbox hat with net flowing around her eyebrows. Having missed the circus act we had just performed, and completely oblivious to my predicament, I heard one say very loudly to the other (I'm not sure which was hard of hearing): "Oh no, Agnes, I don't want any yarn today. I've got enough yarn to last me for two years!"

That statement really sank in. I stopped dead in my tracks and started to giggle. As I looked at those two old ladies picking through the yarn and then back at my whimpering children, I got a flash of inspiration that was the answer to the question I had just asked myself, "What in the world are you doing with all of these kids!" I knew exactly what I was doing. I was teaching and learning and shaping little lives. I had good health and I could walk fast and I had something to look forward to each day besides knitting. I was suddenly *so* happy that I was in my shoes and not their boots!

G. K. Chesterton said, "The reason the angels can fly is that they have learned how to take themselves lightly." This is one of my favorite things to remember when life's crises seem to be too much of a burden or I become overly anxious. One of the great surprises of motherhood is how much humor lightens the load. Life can get serious, but I think truly, in perspective, it's mostly funny. Start writing and keep laughing!

Surprise Nineteen

The Hardest Part Is Taking Care
of Yourself: To Eat or Not to Eat . . .
That Is the Question

I guess I have a naturally slow metabolism. I'm grasping at straws, trying to make excuses for the fact that I hate to exercise. Logically, I know how important it is. Exercise strengthens bones, slows aging, cuts down on the chances for heart disease and cancer, and makes you feel better physically and mentally. But one of life's great struggles for me has been to do something about it.

One year I decided to let my body know that I was still there. After years of feeling tied to a new baby, feeding the mobs, cleaning, clearing, and washing, I resolved that the time had come to take care of me! Even though we were still up most nights with our two-year-old and Richard was gone a fair amount, I had older children who could listen for the kids if I left early for some exercise.

The day came when I decided that I was about to change. Early in the morning I got up and pulled on my new tennis shoes, then decided the room would be easier to come back to if I first made the bed and put a few things away. On the way down the stairs, I saw a pile of dirty clothes half in and half out of a stuffed hamper and decided my day would go smoother if I threw in a load of washing, which could be done by the time I got back. On the way through the kitchen I realized that I could go on a longer walk and not worry about getting back if I put breakfast on the table first. On the way through the family room, with great chagrin, I noticed that the leftovers from the "video party" the night before were strewn everywhere. Shoes and socks, pillows and cups, as well as a fine sprinkling of popcorn covered the floor. I stopped to clean it up lest someone should come by while I was gone and think this was the home of the garbage pail kids. Just as I was stepping to the door, someone called with a list of girls for Girls Camp and wanted to know if I could relay a message to each of them about what they were supposed to pack and get back to her within half an hour.

By the time I finished that, the two-year-old was up, crying to be changed and fed; our six-year-old was begging me to read with him so he could reach his goal for the week; and I had to referee several arguments. The day continued in a similar pattern, and by night my new tennis shoes were covered with peanut butter instead of dirt from speed walking.

That evening, with a cloud of martyrdom hanging around me, I realized that in order ever to have time for myself, I would truly have to *prioritize* myself. I had to put me first. Learning to discipline myself to leave the bed unmade, walk past the messes, let the kids make their own breakfast if need be, and walk past the ringing phone three mornings a week was a true trial!

Survive I did, however, and by the end of the summer I felt better physically than I had for years. The children noticed that I got out my witch hat and broom less often, and Richard (who had been trying to get me to do this for years, but had no idea what it took to get there) was proud!

I wish that that was the end of the story, but unfortunately it is not. Here's an entry from my journal from just two years later:

Exercise . . . ugh! I've tried to like it . . . but I don't. Through the years I have always put exercise nearly last on my list of priorities. Everything seems more important, more pressing, more urgent. When I was a young mother, it seemed that I was always pregnant or nursing. (I was always so worried about exercising when I was pregnant, other than running up and down the stairs 50 times a day and bending over to pick things up at least 100 times. I worried that if I exercised when I was pregnant, my tummy muscles would "learn" that position and never recover.)

However, this year, I feel that I'm starting to deteriorate. That, along

with a back injury from a car accident four years ago, has made me real-
ize that exercise is the only way out of my miserable physical condition.
Richard has been begging me to do something about my aching back
now for years. I know he's mostly concerned for my own good, but I'm
sure he'd like to have a wife who looks good and lasts a while too.

Last Christmas my best present to him was a solemn commitment to do
something about taking care of my body. So—off to the weight rooms
and a trainer I did go, hating every minute on the bike, the StairMaster,
and the weight machines. The first few days I was so stiff that I could
barely smile, but I'll be darned if I don't feel better, look better, and
walk better—after the agony is over. I still resent the time it takes from
important things like grocery shopping and cleaning out the closets and
drawers; but despite the fact that I hate every minute of it, I have the feel-
ing that I'm doing the right thing!

Just reading back through those two incidents makes me feel like a broken record.

I bet you think that now is when I'm going to tell you that I got everything all worked out and that I'm just an exerciseaholic. Not! I do go through periodic spurts of being really good about exercising. I do especially well when I don't have tremendous pressures from kids' needs or making TV shows or writing deadlines. But that is almost never. I've decided, though, that each burst of dedication helps to keep my body pretty well oiled. I've also realized that I am extremely blessed genetically to have a naturally healthy body. Maybe if I was worse off, I'd be better about doing more.

Unfortunately, exercise is not the only thing a body needs to be healthy. One must also eat well. Just as I say how blessed I am to have a healthy body, I am ready to complain about my slow metabolism. As we all know, life isn't fair! As long as I can remember, I have been either dieting or worrying about not dieting. I must consciously decide whether or not to eat each mouthful of food. (Too often I consciously decide . . . to do so.)

The most crushing part for me in dealing with this dilemma is that I live with a very tall, naturally thin person. When we were first married and he was a struggling student at the Harvard Business School and I was teaching school, I would come home from work and cook a casserole for six. I ate one portion and he would easily polish off the other five. It is as easy for him to metabolize food as it is for me to touch the fast-forward button on the VCR when I want to get ahead fast. It just happens. Through the years, as he was munching on his fifth meal at midnight, finishing up with a big chocolate brownie while my stomach churned and begged for some, I have been rubbing my hands with glee all these years, waiting for the day that Richard's metabolism would slow down and he would finally have to go through what I've been going through. I'm still waiting.

He did go on a diet with me one year—for twelve hours. It was disgusting. He just couldn't resist his late night snack. The real blow came the next morning when he found he had lost seven pounds—mostly water—but I was furious and totally overcome by the unfairness of life.

In the old college days I used to be able to drop that extra five pounds by starving a few days—but not any more! The moment I start starving, my fat cells start screaming at each other: "She's trying it again—hang on to every milligram you've got!" And they do! No matter how long I starve, their will is stronger than mine. So, it's onto the old "tons of fruits and vegetables, lots of protein, and no-fat diet." The problem is that I now have ten pounds to lose every year.

Dieting has always been a quandary for me. Somehow it seems so easy to be fully committed to a sensible, nonfat diet at night. Just before I fall asleep, I resolve to sticking to 1,000 calories a day, with lots of vegetables, some fruit and protein, and leaving out the fat. I'm sure I can do it. However, morning comes and the French toast with butter and syrup looks so good, and I really don't have time to make a separate breakfast anyway.

By lunchtime, I'm thinking that I can eat a little "treat" with my lunch because it's what you eat after 6:00 P.M. that really makes the difference. But by 6:00 P.M. things get so crazy—kids going every which direction—and I sometimes forget to eat until after the dust has settled, by which time I am starving and simply cannot resist the cookies the kids are making, dough and all!

"Oh well," I think. "I'm really going to do better tomorrow. You have to enjoy life a little!" And so it goes.

What I have decided over the years is that, like everything else, diet and exercise require a nice balance. Not only in how you diet and exercise, but in how you deal with it. I would like to be as motivated as Jane Fonda and all the machine geeks I saw in the exercise rooms, and I'd love to just eat fruits and vegetables and grains all the time. I do admire those who do. But I can't completely change my mind. I have made some changes for the good, yet my life just isn't complete without at least one little sweet thing a day. What I've finally decided for me is that there is a time to diet and a time not to diet and be happy about it.

There are certain times when eating healthy food and getting sufficient exercise are more crucial than they are at other times. Pregnant and nursing mothers have extreme physical demands placed on their bodies. Eating well and exercising in moderation is the best thing you can do for yourself and your baby. Since I knew that I wanted a large family, I was very meticulous about taking good care of my body for several months before I got pregnant as well as throughout the pregnancy and until I quit nursing the baby. This is the most physically demanding time of a woman's life. It is also an especially frustrating time, because what you eat also affects your child, and a crash diet is out of the question. The baby needs the nutrients more than you do!

Although some pregnancies I managed to get through without feeling overweight and flabby, each pregnancy made it a little harder to maintain my balance. Often I just felt like a miserable fat "blob" the whole time I was nursing a baby, until I was able to do something about it. Some years it took a long time to motivate myself to get back in good shape.

Now finished with my "baby years" (not without much ado, I might add), I have again realized that there are times to rejoice in being on a diet and looking good in your clothes, and times to rejoice in *not* being on a diet and really enjoying a piece of cheesecake without a guilt trip.

Yes, taking care of our physical bodies is one of the great challenges of our lives. Yet these physical bodies are our most treasured earthly possession. The condition they're in often affects every other part of our life. They are given to us that we might feel joy. May we all—especially me—find the proper balance in our physical lives to enjoy them to the fullest and rejoice!

Surprise Twenty
One of the Habits of a Highly Effective Mother Is Simplification

Every mother develops her own way of doing things. From the day we bring that first baby home, we begin to develop habits. Many habits are a result of what our mothers did, or the kind of person we are. Others are just methods we've learned in order to survive. As the multiplicity of children and accompanying complications of life became a part of the fabric of my life, I grew to admire the writings of two people immensely. First, Anne Morrow Lindbergh, especially her *Gift from the Sea*. I felt that she had walked my walk and talked my talk. The other was Henry David Thoreau, who wrote *Walden*. I guess I like what he wrote because it personified what I wanted—what I thought was the ideal: "Our life is frittered away by detail . . . simplify, simplify." he wrote. I know what he said was right, but I also know that Thoreau didn't have nine children—five in braces, three in Scouts, five piano players, two violinists, a cellist, and a harpist. He didn't have PTA meetings, dinners for ten to fifteen every night, and nine basketball games to get children to each week during "the season," which seems to last forever. Yet, though it sometimes seems impossible, simplifying, which both of these authors advocate, is still the answer to many of our pressing problems.

Through watching the media and "the Joneses," we somehow have the impression that our children should have the opportunity to experience everything, all the time. Several years ago, I found that our lives were a disaster because of soccer. We had four boys playing on four different teams, each with one practice and one game per week. Practices were always at dinnertime, so no one saw much of anyone else. Dinner was just a quick refueling, two or three bodies at a time. At the end of the season, I sat all the boys down, looked them straight in the eye, and said, "Boys, I hope this doesn't come as too much of a shock. Dad and I have talked this over and we know you may be upset, but our family life has been disrupted so much by soccer that we have decided that you're not going to be playing soccer in the spring." Amazingly, instead of tears, I got actual smiles. One of the boys volunteered, "That's okay, Mom, we don't really like soccer anyway!" What a blow! All my time, energy, gas, and frustration spent on something they didn't like anyway. Boy, do I wish I'd asked sooner!

Since then we've simplified to two sports (basketball in winter, tennis in summer). And we do all the orthodontist appointments on the same day.

The lives of most people in America today are cluttered with too many "things." We have a friend who is an advertising executive. He claims the average American is exposed to three to four hundred advertising messages per day—all begging us to think we *need* things we actually only *want*. Even those who can least afford it are duped into filling their lives with unnecessary things.

Having fallen at least partially into the same pit, we are often glad that we move as frequently as we do. It allows us to get rid of tons of excess things. I can't believe the amount of junk we can collect in just a few years. There were broken toys that we kept thinking we would mend, puzzles with missing pieces that we *knew* we would find as soon as we threw them away. There were books with torn pages that I rationalized someday the children might want to save. There were clothes no one had worn for years and "early-marriage" furniture that we were emotionally attached to. Finally, we decided to part with the whole collection. As we sort through things, our rule of thumb is: If you haven't used it for a year, give it to someone who will. It feels *so* good!

When we returned to Washington, D.C., after a few years in the West, we took less than half of our furniture and found that we got along beautifully. Our home is much smaller there, and I found to my delight that the housework was cut in half. Living without so much "stuff" taught me a lesson. We decided that when it was back-to-school time, we would advocate that each child have just one new outfit to wear the first day of school, instead of worrying about a whole new wardrobe. (I have to say that this worked best when our children were small.) They were perfectly happy to wear their summer shorts for a while and simplify their wardrobe. Teenagers are a little different.

I used to think I had to have elaborate birthday parties for each of the children or they would think I didn't love them. I laugh when I remember crying over the littered stairs one day two hours before a three-year-old's birthday party. I was nine months pregnant and having regular contractions. I can't imagine what could have been in my mind. I guess I was so afraid that a mother would come in and notice, or that those three-year-olds would think I was a terrible housekeeper. I finally got on the phone and hired a neighborhood teenager to come in and vacuum. After years of learning to simplify, I now know that, first, I should never have vacuumed before the party no matter what . . . only *after;* second, there are a hundred easier, simpler ways to have a party than at your own home. Little kids love going out—even if it's to the dollar movie theaters. Going *anywhere* is a party!

Speaking of getting help, having household help (which I resisted for years not only for financial reasons but also for reasons of pride) is a wonderful idea. During the school year I have two ladies that clean like crazy for three hours. It is heaven! I've decided that I'd rather have a cleaning lady and drive an old clunker than have a Lexus, any day. It frees up your time and your mind. Even though just ten minutes after they leave, it often looks exactly like it did ten minutes before the cleaning ladies came, something about knowing that the bathrooms have been done and the kitchen floor has been mopped is a great stress reducer and simplifier.

Richard loves turning around old clichés so much that he has written a book about it. He worries about those of us who have the old cliché rattling around in our heads that goes: "If a thing is worth doing, it's worth doing well." He believes that there are just a few things really worth doing well. Most of them have to do with relationships with people and with nature. There are another ton of things worth doing, but just barely . . . like keeping an immaculate house or killing yourself over something just to make a good impression. "Big Daddy" advocates turning the old cliché around and instead saying, "If a thing is just barely worth doing, then just barely do it!" He has taught me well. I like to write that little message in the dust on my piano. It reminds me of another old saying: "An immaculate house is the sign of a wasted life."

As mothers, and especially women, we often create our own crises because we don't simplify. When we decide to host a party or someone asks us to make a poster to advertise the youth activity at church, we throw ourselves into it as though our life depends upon it. Our reputation and pride are at stake, and we kill ourselves to do a fabulous job, even at the expense of our family.

Make simplifying a game this month. See how much you can sacrifice without giving up the things you really love. Simplify meals and cleanup on busy days with paper plates, and yes, even use convenience foods. Often at work, we even "make-work" by doing things in a much more time-consuming and elaborate way than is necessary. Simplify errands by finding ways to cut out those that aren't absolutely necessary, and by combining them with other runs. Simplify toys by getting rid of or at least putting away the ones your children don't love. Don't buy toys with thousands of pieces until their owners can take care of them. Give the children more Scotch tape and paper to create with.

Simplifying is especially effective if you are under a lot of pressure and desperate to change. The key is really just using mental energy to think about the problems. Analyze the complications of your life, then think what you can do to simplify them. You'll be amazed how many of the things you think are "have-to's" are really "choose-to's." Making a habit of simplifying can be one of a mother's best habits. Remember the principle of "pizzazz" as you simplify. There is a fine line between simplifying and becoming mediocre. Use your creativity and do things with flair but in its simplest form. Life may take on new meaning!

Surprise Twenty-One
PMS Makes Witches; or,
I'm Not Okay, You're Not Okay

There is some controversy over exactly what PMS is. In this chapter I am not talking about intricate medical terms. I am referring to the hormonal imbalance that occurs in most women in one way or another according to their hormone levels during monthly cycles and pregnancies, which prompts them to react in different, sometimes irrational ways.

Some women are affected to extremes and are plagued by these imbalances each month. Others hardly notice a change. A T-shirt that sticks in my memory and made me chuckle was one that a normal-looking woman was wearing one day at Arby's. It said: "Watch Out! I'm dealing with PMS and I have a GUN!" On the other hand, a friend with eight small children and seemingly endless patience tells me that she had PMS once . . . just an uneasy feeling that things were not right. She felt depressed and out of control for no apparent reason. Alarmed, she immediately called her doctor, who explained the symptoms of PMS, which fit her perfectly. She was so relieved that she wasn't going crazy!

Once when Richard and I were doing a series of TV shows on the family, we were scheduled to do one called "Eliminating Anger from Your Life." Our guest was a distinguished professor and counselor. On the way to the show, I spouted, "We can't be serious about doing a show about eliminating anger! I'm sure one can control anger, but I have doubts about actual elimination. One thing is certain: This man has certainly never had PMS!" Richard smiled and quickly agreed, lest he should upset my hormones.

Just that week I had stomped into the kitchen wearing my witch hat and broom while all the children were sitting at the breakfast table. I was already furious about how the day had gone so far. Absolutely no one had done anything they were supposed to have done. No beds were made, no practicing was done; yet these chattering little "good-for-nothings," who had been so cute last week, dared to be giggling at the breakfast table as though everything was perfectly okay. With smoke almost visibly curling out of my ears, hormone-unbalanced and definitely *not* okay, I began yelling at the kids uncharacteristically loudly and menacingly.

"I can't believe what has happened this morning—absolutely nothing! It is beyond my ability to understand why you have to have somebody screaming at you every minute in order to get anything done around here," I raved. Some of the children looked shocked; others amazed; one maybe even a little scared. But the one with big, brown eyes and a grin on his face began to giggle.

"Noah, don't you dare laugh at me when I'm this angry! You're taking your life in your hands!" I shouted. Seven-year-old Talmadge leaned his head over on sixteen-year-old Saren's shoulder and began laugh too. Suddenly, it was as though someone had uncorked some laughing gas. They were all tittering . . . just as if they were watching a funny movie. As the blinding truth finally sank in, I realized that they *were* watching a funny movie . . . starring me . . . and co-starring PMS!

I guess the kids have learned to deal with my hormone imbalances because their father handles them pretty well himself. By about the third pregnancy, when I would get angry and start telling Richard what an insensitive, stupid, lazy, unthinking oaf he was, he had learned how to respond. Instead of overreacting or coming back with his own list of nasty names, he would stop, register in his brain what was happening, and say, usually with a smile, "You don't mean that. I know you don't mean that. Just wait an hour [or until morning] and you'll realize that you really don't mean all those things."

At first, his smile made me even more angry and I would vehemently insist that I did mean it! I really *did!* However, usually when time had passed, I came to my senses and realized that he was once again a great guy. My hormones were just a little tipsy.

Every mother has her own way of dealing with PMS and hormone imbalances. Our reactions are all different because we are dealing with different problems . . . different husbands, different children, different pressures, different perceptions.

One of the most valuable lessons of my life has been to learn not to judge. Yet this lesson, which I remember my father teaching me when I was a child, is still one that I have to keep relearning and reminding myself of. We tend to judge others by how we feel or how we would react, without knowing the details. When I used to hear of women being depressed, I had a quick solution: Snap out of it! Although sometimes that is good advice and is sometimes possible, there are certainly times when it is not nearly as easy as it sounds.

As I mentioned earlier, in the past five years my aging mother has broken her pelvis twice. Each time she was able to cope with the physical recovery with flying colors, even though it was very difficult. However, her mental and emotional recovery was much more difficult. She began to think that her life as she had known it was over and that she would never be the same. Next came panic attacks and major depression. Her body chemistry was definitely out of balance. I could see after working with her day after day for several weeks that she was not going to just "snap out of it." I began reading books and understanding the fine line that our body and soul teeter on each day. For her, medications created worse side effects. It took thousands of hours of trying new things before she began to feel normal again. Through sheer grit, medication, common sense, weighing advice to fit her particular body, and lots of faith and help from heaven, she did come back. I now have a new, healthy respect for the word "depression." It is real, extremely complicated, and treatable.

The biggest problem that I see in dealing with PMS and hormone imbalances is that if not understood, they can begin to affect our self-esteem. We are angry with ourselves for being irritable and irrational, which carries over into other parts of our life. Often hormones fluctuate so that something that drives you crazy one day doesn't even faze you the next. Taking into account that there are going to be some days when you just feel that you're not okay and that nobody else is okay either, it might not be a bad idea to say to yourself or whoever is affected by your bad mood, "Hold on. I don't think I meant that. Check with me tomorrow." Forgive yourself, and go on. If that down mood doesn't go away, get some help. There is a wide range of therapy, from medical to spiritual, which can change the way the world looks to you.

We did do the TV show that day. Dr. Terry Olsen talked about eliminating anger, and it was very interesting. First, by using examples from a live audience, he pointed out that we have a natural tendency to blame others for making us angry. As I thought about my own angry feelings the past week, I knew he was certainly right about that. I was always mad at a circumstance, something that seemed out of my control, and silly situations that other people (particularly my children) had created.

Next, we were taught that we must first realize that we are in charge of ourselves. Only we can determine whether we get angry. We may have what we think is a good reason for becoming angry, often under the guise of righteous indignation, but it is usually just a good excuse to be angry.

Dr. Olsen claimed that if we could only stop ourselves just before we launch into our anger and listen to our conscience, it will always tell us the right thing to do. Stopping ourselves in time sounds so simple, but it is the very hardest part. He maintained that if we can just pause long enough to ask, "What does my conscience tell me to do?" and, "Who is really to blame if I lose my temper?" we'll always do the right thing. (Without warning, it popped into my mind that that was exactly what Richard had done when he had reacted positively to my negative comments to him when I was pregnant. That stupid oaf had once again changed into a genius.)

By the end of the taping that day I decided that Dr. Olsen was really absolutely right. If I did what he suggested every single time I was tempted to get angry, I could eliminate my anger. There are just two things he didn't mention. (1) This is not a quick-fix solution, even though it is based on a correct principle. It requires as much time and attention as a weight loss program—training one's mind to work and think a different way and create new habits. And (2) he has never had PMS!

Surprise Twenty-Two
You Have to Keep Reminding Yourself
How Much Fun You're Having

"This baby is so helpless and heavy. When he learns to walk, I'm really going to start enjoying life," we say to ourselves. When he does start walking, we say, "Remember those great days when the baby just sat in one place and I always knew where he was!"

"Just think of the fun we're going to have when the children are gone," we conclude at the height of our parenting years. Then, when they're gone, we long for the days when they were young. "Those days when the children were home were the happiest days of my life," we mourn.

It's so easy to live life in the past or the future. Just yesterday, I said to Richard, "I will be so glad when I get this book done." He smiled that you-know-what's-coming-next smile and asked, "But aren't you having fun doing it?" I had to admit that I was.

Somehow, the future and the past seem so exciting, but the present . . . we're just trying to get through it. Most days we feel like the little gerbil on his treadmill, running frantically for hours on end. The faster he goes, the faster his world spins. At the end of the day he is exhausted, and he is exactly where he started.

Richard and I have had opportunities to live in what sound like some very exciting circumstances. During the past few years we have become pretty much full-time parents, writers, and speakers. Because we've wanted our children to "broaden and contribute," and since writers can pretty much live anywhere they can buy pencil and paper, we have lived in some fairly strange places.

Occasionally, we have taken the children out of school for periods of time or put them in "different" schools in England, New England, or Virginia, but usually our wild adventures are during the summers. We spent two summers building a log cabin in the wilderness of Oregon. Once we took the children to live in a mountain village in Mexico. Another summer we spent in Japan and the Philippines. In 1992, we took seven of the kids to work in an orphanage for handicapped children in Romania.

Of course, looking back on all that now, those were the greatest experiences of our lives. But as committed as I thought I was to enjoying the present, I spent a lot of time during each adventure wishing for the past or the future.

My greatest asset the first summer we attempted to build the log cabin, about ninety miles from the nearest town in the Blue Mountains of Oregon, was that I had never been camping in my life. So I didn't know what to expect. Our oldest children were young teenagers and the youngest was not quite two. By ten o'clock each morning, this baby looked like he had been rolled in honey and dipped in dirt. For our water supply, we ran PVC piping from a mountain spring a hundred yards from the site we had chosen for the cabin. Yearning for privacy, the older girls set up a tent of their own. The rest of us lived in a huge tepee, although lots of nights we just slept under the magnificent firmament of stars.

Once a week, we made the journey into the nearest town an hour and a half away for groceries. Our "refrigerator" was either the coolers with ice or a hole we scooped out in the ground and filled with the constantly flowing ice water from the spring. We cooked over a fire in big dutch ovens and learned to love campfire dinners and "smores" (graham crackers with melted marshmallows and chocolate—great for my diet!). The second summer we were there, we had a cast-iron stove and we cooked like our pioneer ancestors.

During the days, the children and I spent so many hours skinning logs that we could see skinned trunks every time we closed our eyes.

Even with all that fun and excitement, after the first two weeks I found myself longing for a hot shower or at least a warm tub full of clean water that I could dip the baby in every few minutes. It seemed that I spent most of my time thinking about what to feed everybody next, and I began to resent the fact that I spent so much time cooking or heating water to do the dishes. I loved not having a phone or a TV or a herd of the children's friends under my feet, but I found myself remembering the ease of the old days with the dishwasher and Wendy's. Some mornings I had to shake myself to remember how much fun I was having.

Our summer in Mexico was looked forward to with great anticipation. We had visions of our children all learning Spanish and enjoying living in a wonderful new culture. In actuality, some things were even better than we had planned. We had two darling maids, who adored our baby and who cleaned everything from top to bottom every day and ironed everything right down to our socks.

But for reasons too complicated to explain here, we didn't have a car. We either walked everywhere we went or hired nine horses (the little kids doubled with Richard and me) to take us for a stroll through the village. We thought we were going to observe the townspeople. As it turned out, we were the best parade they'd ever seen. They giggled at the "gringos" passing through their cobblestone streets as they sat on the front steps of their houses, whose square footage was about the same as our laundry room at home. Occasionally a newfound taxi driver friend would allow all eleven of us to cram into his taxi to take a ride in the countryside or to go shopping in Guadalajara, which was about an hour away. About half an hour of sweating all over each other in that un-air-conditioned taxi, we were pinching ourselves to remember how much fun we were having.

By the end of our sojourn there, the children had all learned a few sentences in Spanish, but they had also learned that they didn't need a spoken language to communicate with their new Spanish friends. They grew to love one happy little girl who came every day to watch them swim. Even though they begged her to join them in our pool, she stood barefoot and in the same dress every day and just watched. Finally, on the last day, she jumped into the pool in her dress. Suddenly we realized that not only did she not have a swimsuit, she didn't have any other dress. Nor did she own a pair of shoes.

After several weeks, we again began to complain about the present. Everybody was tired of having diarrhea, and I couldn't imagine how I could explain to a Mexican doctor who could only understand a few words of English that I needed medication for a yeast infection. It was hard enough to figure out what was in the cans of food at the grocery story with their Spanish labels, let alone to find the proper medication in a funny-looking pharmacy. We were soaking our fruits and vegetables in Clorox water and worrying about everything we ate. One day we found a beetle in the bottom of one of the huge bottles of purified water we had just drunk. We reminded ourselves again of how much fun we'd had. The children had learned that you don't have to have shoes to be happy. So we went home.

Several years later, a very kind, middle-aged American couple invited all eleven of us to spend a month with them in Japan. By then our oldest children were attending college in Boston, but they didn't want to miss the adventure. (Thank goodness for frequent-flyer miles.) "How exciting and educational!" we exclaimed. We looked forward to a marvelous experience in this mystical, faraway land of people who, at that point in history, looked as though they were about to take over the world financially.

Our friends had a huge home by Japanese standards and were able to offer a tatami room for the girls, one for the boys, and a separate little room with a mattress on the floor for Richard and me. Their house rented for $12,000 a month. (They paid $1,000 and their company paid the other $11,000.)

It was a truly magnificent experience. Each child had a chance to go to a Japanese school with children their own age. They had an opportunity to do a Japanese sand painting in the home of the priestess whose husband cared for the very old and historic forty-foot statue of Buddha in Kamakura, the ancient capital of Japan, where we lived. We grew attached to a wonderful neighborhood of the kindest, most gift-giving people we had ever met, who were bewildered by the complexities of this crazy huge family from America. In turn, we were amazed at the complexity of their lives . . . each meal having several courses that required many complicated steps to prepare. Even cooking rice was complicated. We never ceased to be astonished at the number of ways they could prepare rice . . . or squid.

We walked a thousand miles up and down steep hills. One Japanese neighbor, who spoke good English, took us on field trips to wonderful Japanese gardens, the Nissan auto-assembly factory, bamboo forests, Buddhist temples, and a long tunnel which monks had dug out with their fingers during a war.

But once again, we found that there were difficulties. A gallon of milk cost $5. Apples and carrots were $1 each and hamburger $5 a pound. That was the cheap stuff. We found watermelons for $85 and cantaloupes for $60. An orange fishhead for a special kind of soup ran about $75. Even rice was outrageously priced. Squid was pretty reasonable, but it was something we hadn't acquired a taste for. There was a neighborhood food co-op where we could order food in bulk once a week. All the neighbors came out to see us pick up our order on Wednesdays. It was like going to the circus for them.

I felt keenly aware of the fact that we were in someone else's home. We cooked for our hosts, since it would be absurd for them to cook for us. After everyone was asleep, I made sure that every crumb was picked up, all the fingerprints were removed, and that the shoes were lined neatly up at the door for the following day. Some nights I found myself scrubbing shoes for the children who were scheduled to go to school the next day, as each child was required to have one pair of outdoor shoes and a spotlessly clean pair for indoor wear. Slippers were provided in some schools, but our children's feet, which are notoriously big even by American standards, just wouldn't fit in them. We had a fabulous experience, but we could hardly wait to get home!

Probably our most memorable trip was to the Romanian orphanage. We had friends whose family had gone the previous summer to work at an orphanage in Bucharest. This particular summer, they had two orphanages that they were interested in assisting, and thought we could help them.

They were doing extensive painting and fixing up in one and wondered if we could take over in the other one. Since we had one daughter already there doing humanitarian service and missionary work in

Romania, we decided that it would be a great experience for everyone. (Again, thank goodness for frequent-flyer miles.)

Like a Fourth of July parade, we left with a duffel bag for our own clothes and twenty-four huge suitcases full of toys, clothes, and diapers for the orphanage. One son had taken the opportunity to use this good cause for his Eagle project and we were stuffed with every imaginable thing for these unfortunate children in Romania.

A whole book could be written about what we learned, what we saw, and what fun we had in that small orphanage in a dirty, smoggy little town in the Transylvanian Alps, not far from Count Dracula's castle. The joy of seeing a small child, whose previous playground toys were gravel and broken glass, experience his first ride on a big wheel just can't be described. The sheer ecstasy on another child's face when he saw a new book or was placed on a little chair with a crown on his head and told that he was unique and special was a lot more than fun. Fifty little children aged three to eight who slept in two rooms, dressed in shambles, and seldom saw the outside world provided us more "fun" than we had thought possible.

On the other hand, there were the days when we ran out of granola bars and peanut butter and were living on eggs and bread and pork steaks, sometimes with flies attached, in hotel dining rooms where we had to step over cat droppings on the way to the tables. There were the days when, after sweltering at the hot little orphanage, painting walls, and holding darling children who were consistently wetting on us, we had to remind each other vigorously how much fun we were having as the hotel management informed us that evening that they were sorry, but even the promised two hours of hot water each morning and evening had been suspended. Although the joys of our journey far outweighed the trials, we found ourselves looking forward to having a hot shower any time we wanted.

Two weeks later, back in my own laundry room, as I sorted a mountain of socks in considerable pain because of splits in both thumbs from constant contact with antibacterial soap and cleaning fluids at the orphanage. I always seemed to have painful hangnails and splits in my thumbs and tried to console myself, while painfully turning socks inside out and folding them together. On this particular day as I was feeling sorry for myself, I noticed a counted cross-stitch sign that I had purposely hung on the wall to read as I labored at my least favorite job. It said: "Reasons to Rejoice." I realized right away that no matter how good our past or future may be, there is always a reason to rejoice in the present. I rejoiced that I *had* hands and that next I was going to use them to drive the middle school car pool, and then to eat frozen yogurt on the way home. Those reasons to rejoice help us to remember how much fun we're having . . . today.

Surprise Twenty-Three
What It Is Really Important to Worry About Is Often Not What You Think

I am really quite a good professional worrier. I got this gift from my dad, who I remember clearly worried about a lot of things, although I can't remember what any of them were. I worry about the earthquake and hurricane victims, about abused children, unwed mothers, and homeless families. I worry about the people in wartorn countries and about those being tortured in dark, dank prisons in South America. Mostly, I worry about my kids.

I am somewhat comforted to realize that I'm not the only one who worries. One day while waiting for our preschoolers to finish a morning session at Joy School, I overheard a small group of mothers discussing their worries.

With chin cradled in hand, I leaned forward and listened:

"I am so worried about my four-year-old," one young mother said. "He is still sucking his thumb. Just thinking about the other kids teasing him over it during kindergarten recess makes me feel sick!"

"Well, my two-year-old is sleeping with us every night," another chimed in. "It's kind of like sleeping with a soggy, twenty-five pound toy powered by an Eveready battery. He just keeps wiggling and wriggling!"

"Feel lucky," confided a third young mother. "My three-year-old is emotionally attached to his Superman cape. He wears it morning, noon, and night, to church, to preschool, and screams for it the entire time he's in the tub. I have to sneak into his room once a week after he's asleep, and wash and dry it and get it back on him before he wakes up, or he's a basket case."

Listening in on this "worry session" of young mothers made me remember when one of our toddlers was driving me insane. Most people with eighteen-month-olds will identify with playing in the toilet. Almost every child by the time he is two has dumped numberless rolls of toiler paper down the john. The fact that with very little effort they can gleefully roll out minutes of entertainment makes toilet play almost irresistible.

But we had a son who went even further. He didn't stop with just flopping his hand in the water like a mother testing the bath temperature; he actually climbed *into* the toilet! In the morning before I had time to get him dressed, he was in there, diaper and all. By afternoon he was in there again, clothes, shoes, socks, and all (regardless of what else was in there). It was ghastly.

We tried everything from scolding to spanking, but absolutely *nothing* worked except keeping the bathroom door closed. Alas! The only thing harder than getting kids to flush is teaching them to remember to close the bathroom door. Inevitably, at least once a day and often three or four times, I would find him in one of the four toilets in the house, squealing with delight as he made toilet plunging noises, squatted like an Indian, and moved his body up and down. It was like he was in his own private swimming pool while hanging onto the toilet seat as a tiny inner tube. By six o'clock, he was out of clothes and I was out of patience. By his bedtime, I was exhausted from running around, checking all the bathroom doors or changing his soaking clothes (which were hard to peel off), and extracting his soggy shoes, which was kind of like removing a suction cup from a mirror. For about nine months it seemed that I did nothing but change wet clothes and check on bathroom doors. Even when we went out to a restaurant or a movie, my mind was totally preoccupied wondering if the baby-sitter had closed the bathroom door!

Remembering those harried days made me smile while writing about it one day. And then suddenly I realized something amazing: I couldn't remember which child it was who was our "toilet swimmer." I honestly couldn't remember! This worry had been something that occupied my thoughts day after day for months, and now I couldn't remember for all the money in the world which child it was.

After initial panic about Alzheimer's disease (or old-timer's disease, as our children call it), I couldn't help giggling. "Old-timers" aside, I realized that forgetting what we worried about is one of the gifts of motherhood. In retrospect, not only do we forget who did what, but we also realize that most things we spent considerable time worrying and fretting about aren't really worth expending all that energy on. Kids usually turn out all right in spite of weird idiosyncrasies anyway.

When I got home, I asked the older children who the "toiletmonger" was, and they reminded me that it was Noah. Of course, Noah! Who else would spend all his time in an "ark" with the water *inside?* Noah is our self-assured, friendly, thirteen-year-old goal setter, whose greatest gift is his tenacity to accomplish what he wants to do—like a Doberman guard dog with his teeth sunk into the seat of the pants of a robber and not about to let go. Noah will not quit until he gets what he wants. And usually what he wants now is not to swim in the toilet, but to get good grades. If only I had known that Noah's determination to get what he wanted would translate from getting into the toilet to setting goals and reaching them, I would have been saved so much worry and time! Often what we term strange behavior in a two-year-old is only a manifestation of a positive trait that will work for him in later life. Of course we can't say, "Don't worry," because worrying is part of being a mother. But we can say, "Don't worry too much," because eccentricity is part of being a child as they figure out how to become an adult.

I must say that in retrospect, I have become much more flexible in worrying about what the children eat. I started almost obsessively worried about our children eating too much candy. I absolutely abhorred the ever present candy and gum at every check-out stand in America, and was resolutely firm in adhering to my policy of not allowing candy in any of my children's hands except on Saturdays. By about the sixth child, I had softened. In fact, I had decided that bribery was the best policy, and offered them anything they wanted at the check-out if they'd just be quiet.

At one point, I spent considerable time worrying about the eating habits of our thirteen-year-old. Her idea of great food was Twinkies, Ding Dongs, licorice, and white bread with no crust squashed up into a ball. Again in retrospect, I should have realized that it would be hard to imagine her as a mother with her future little children following behind her in the grocery story begging and pleading, "Please, Mommy, no more Ding Dongs. Can we *please* just have some lettuce!"

Our children's safety is one thing that most parents spend a considerable amount of time worrying about. I don't worry much about that personally because Richard does it all for me. He insists on knowing where every child is at every moment. If a child is out of contact for more than two hours, Richard is absolutely certain that she has been kidnapped. He's the type that lays in bed at night and worries that our toddler is going to get up while he was sleeping, climb up on the kitchen counter, put her chubby little foot down the garbage disposal, and accidentally turn it on. With a worrier like that in the house, I don't have to worry nearly as much.

On a more serious note, there are, of course, some legitimate reasons to worry about raising children in our society. With violence, sexual experimentation, peer pressure to use drugs and alcohol, and negative media influences knocking on our door at every turn, we feel frightened and trapped, and sometimes clueless to know what to do to keep our children from harm. Thus we come to the real core of the matter: What it is *really* important to worry about.

Several years ago, Richard and I decided to quit spending so much time worrying about all the negative possibilities in our children's lives. Instead, we determined we should be worrying more about giving them tools that will serve as an defensive armor as they faced those negatives. This required more than showing them a video about the danger of strangers. It meant having dinner together and finding a systematic way to teach basic, universal values. The result was a book called *Teaching Your Children Values,* which you may want to refer to if you need help. We are still actively involved in this endless endeavor. Of course, this is not a magic potion, and we still worry about children getting into situations beyond their control. But having "armed" them with protective inner values, we don't worry about our children's choices as much as we used to when they were tiny and the world seemed like a fire-spitting dragon ready to devour an unsuspecting child. I like what Roy Disney said: "It's not hard to make decisions when you know what your values are."

Other things I used to worry about included our house and how it looked, and where it was and what the wallpaper looked like. I used to wish for a bigger house and an enormous yard for the children. I do believe that you create your environment and then your environment creates you. Your well-being does have to do partly with feeling comfortable with where you live. But through the years, I've decided that I really didn't want a huge, gorgeous house on a spacious lot to be happy. In fact, we began to realize that too big a house and too much stuff would limit our freedom and take up too much time and attention. When we finally reached a reasonable level of financial comfort (which took many years in a relatively small house for nine kids), we decided to save our money for things that were more important to us than a glitzy house, like travel and other smaller places in different locations where we could get some of the things that our "home base" didn't provide, but which afforded a way to do family things that were bonding and important.

Money and where you live are sometimes touchy and sensitive issues. I have appreciated being on both ends of the spectrum. From struggling for years to make ends meet, to being blessed to be able to buy whatever we really need, the one thing that remains constant is deciding what is really important. At some point I discovered that I really needed to quit worrying about changing what I had and begin worrying about changing what I was—inside. I needed to be dissatisfied enough with my weaknesses to change. My present became much happier. Georgie Anne Geyer said, "Follow what you love. Don't deign to ask what 'they' are looking for out there. Ask what you have inside. Follow not your interests, which change, but what you are and what you love, which will and should not change."

Our nineteen-year-old daughter Saydi recently returned from a study abroad experience in Israel. There she had the luxury of more time to think and ponder her life than she probably will have for the rest of her days. In her last letter home, she came up with a thought that I think is profound: "What we really need to do," she said,

> is constantly keep in mind the things that are really important. We often use the word "priority" to mean putting that which is important first, but I think we sometimes take the word "priority" for granted. If we instead say to ourselves, "What is really important?" we might be better off. It is important to be in touch with ourselves . . . to meditate . . . to read Scripture and other great literature . . . to contemplate life . . . to reach beyond ourselves to become better people . . . to value relationships more than things and to realize the value of helping others along the way. Those are the things that are really important!

I was touched by her wisdom, and I knew that when she reentered the real world of everyday worries, that would be one of her most valuable lessons. When I'm really worried about something, I try to ask myself, Will it matter in five years? My response always puts what needs to be done at the moment in perspective.

Faith, hope, and charity go a long way in helping us know what to worry about. Maybe we should quit worrying about some of our children's idiosyncrasies and worry just enough about their safety to do something positive to combat possible pitfalls. Maybe we should have hope that we can do some small thing to help with the worrisome problems of the world by sending our own kind of aid to the homeless and helpless. Maybe we should quit worrying so much about trying to change the people around us and worry more about changing ourselves.

It takes so much time and energy to worry. Maybe dismissing unfounded worries and looking for help from a higher source to help us deal with genuine worries is what's really important!

Surprise Twenty-Four
Unconditional Love Is Easy,
Not Counting Unconditional "Like"

There is an interesting parallel between dogs and parents. This theory crystallized for me one week last winter. I decided to try to find a copy of *How to Win Friends and Influence People* for a teenager who felt awkward and anxious about his abilities to socialize. That old Dale Carnegie classic had motivated me to say "Hi" to a lot of people when I was a "turned-in" teenager, so of course I assumed that it would save him, too.

Not without effort, I located the book and determined to underline the key passages, as I was quite sure that this sixteen-year-old would probably not receive the idea of reading the whole book with jubilation.

Plowing through the first chapter, I read a story that made me think. To paraphrase, it said that while most domesticated animals provide us with something useful—wool, milk, eggs, and so on—dogs provide only one thing: unconditional love.

"I should be more like a dog," I thought, as a mother who loves her children unconditionally but still thinks of endless ways for them to improve.

Speaking of dogs, that same weekend I attended a dinner party at the home of a former Reagan cabinet member in a posh Washington, D.C., neighborhood and had a fascinating discussion with a beautiful, intelligent woman—the mother of a high-school-age daughter. She seemed flustered when I talked about children, and asked if I didn't think it a good idea to send a teenage girl to a boarding school so she could sort out her problems with other girls her age, and receive a great education while she was about it.

But when the conversation shifted to the subject of dogs, her countenance changed. With great enthusiasm, she spent the rest of the evening telling me about her dogs. They were thoroughbreds that she had adopted because other owners had been unable to control them. She obviously adored dogs. Every March she avidly watched the annual dog show broadcast from New York. She gave a beautiful framed portrait of her husband's favorite dog to him for Christmas.

I found it ironic that she was thinking of sending her child to have someone else take care of while she took care of someone else's troublesome dogs.

After we parted company, I realized that since I love teenagers much more than dogs, I should have offered to take her teenager if she would take our puppy—our Able, a huge, one-year-old chocolate Lab who has destroyed thousands of dollars' worth of furniture, antique Indian rugs, Mom and Dad's beloved leather shoes, and kids' hard-earned basketball shoes.

One week she hurdled the fence which Richard had spent literally hundreds of hours making dog-escape proof. Immediately she ran to a new neighbor's yard—the only people on the block who didn't know her from previous visits. They, of course, quickly called the county dog pound. After three days of hanging flyers on every tree and signpost, and countless searches on bicycles (the seats of which, incidentally, had been chewed to shreds by our dearly beloved Able) and cars (whose upholstery had been gnawed by the same), the dog pound called. She was there. Richard and several boys dashed off to the rescue.

While they stopped at the sign at the end of our dead-end street to look at a map, our neighbor was backing his huge semi-truck full of exercise equipment into our street, didn't see our van, and ripped off most of the metal on the driver's side, exposing what the boys called the interesting "innards" of our hapless vehicle. Luckily the engine was untouched, so the "rescue crew" proceeded to the pound. Poor Able was literally ecstatic with joy at having found her lost family—knocking over kids with the powerful wag of her flailing tail, and depositing drool on every eager face with her soppy tongue, like a one-hundred-pound hummingbird darting from flower to flower to gather nectar.

The Dale Carnegie story about unconditional love popped into my mind as Able burst into our front door with joyous kisses for Charity and me, while one of her young masters struggled with the leash to keep her from overpowering us with love.

Children are also a little like dogs. Yes, they *are* a lot of trouble, but they also almost always feel unconditional love for us. It is so crucial that we express our unconditional love for them. A friend recently told me a story about having a heart-to-heart talk with a teen-aged adopted daughter who had moved out of the house and was living a totally different lifestyle to the other members of the family. She had broken her parents' hearts with her behavior on many occasions. My friend, her mother, said that she looked deep into her daughter's heavily made up eyes one night, the face caked with makeup, black lipstick predominating, her ears pierced in several places, and said, "Jenny, has it ever occurred to you that a loving Heavenly Father sent you to us so that you could learn from us how to conduct your life in order to be happy?" Her rebellious daughter answered with equal sincerity and without malice, "Mother, has it ever occurred to you that I was sent to you so that you could learn to love *all* people?" The question startled my friend, and she realized that it was time to get out the unconditional love.

Yes, there are times when kids do even worse things than Able is able to conjure. Husbands, too! There are lots of days when I have looked Richard in the eye after we've had a misunderstanding or a round with two strong wills clashing, and say, "I still love you, but I don't like you very much right now!" He knows what I mean because he feels the very same way about me.

When kids or husbands make mistakes or get on your nerves and/or exhibit poor judgment or make bad decisions, nothing is more important than saying, "I don't like what you just did, but there is nothing you could do that would make me stop loving you." Wait, don't say that—they'll test you. How about, "What you did makes me angry. I don't like your behavior at all. But you should know that no matter what, I still love you."

Surprise Twenty-Five
Praise Is a Secret Weapon

Of all the parenting methods and manipulations, there is one word that, if used properly, can cause children almost magically to try harder, do better, and want to *be* better. It's almost like a magic potion. For some reason, many of us think that our job description as parents is mostly to find things that children are doing wrong and correct them. We become obsessed with trying to make our children more like we think they should be, more like we wish we had been, or more like what we should be.

Actually, the very opposite strategy works 110 percent better. If we can just wait for our children to do something right and then immediately tell them about it, the change in their behavior is almost miraculous. For years, Richard and I have had this motto: "Catch them doing something right—then use effusive *praise*." William James said, "The deepest principle of human nature is the craving to be appreciated."

In 1987, our family had an opportunity to go back to England for six months. We had lived there from 1976 to 1979 and felt it was a great opportunity to let the younger children experience the wonderful culture the older children had enjoyed while they were there. Those younger ones wondered what kind of favor we were doing them when they entered the austere British Church of England school system, with its rigorous academic requirements, rules, and uniforms. But they did have the opportunity to go on many fascinating field trips, and on weekends we especially enjoyed going to the birthplaces and old haunts of some of our ancestors.

One weekend, I had the rare opportunity to visit Scotland with three of our older children. In the short forty-eight hours we had there, we learned a great deal about Scotland—and about each other.

I was intensely interested to observe, even in that brief amount of time, the fierce love the Scots have, not only for their own "clan" but for their country. Their pride showed everywhere—from the kilted bagpipes to the monuments dedicated to their favorite sons, Sir Walter Scott and David Livingstone. We saw little old ladies practically swoon over the lilting, lyrical melodies of Robert Burns, their beloved songwriter and poet, at the King's Theater in Edinburgh.

The castle guides were full of glowing stories about their heroic Robert the Bruce, their Bonnie Prince Charlie, and their loyal Mary Queen of Scots, even though each of these historical characters was far from perfect.

Coming back to the present and my own little clan, I had envisioned two days of utter bliss without the distractions of the younger children and the baby. (Richard was at home with the youngest six—claiming that he was having a wonderful time when I called on the phone.)

I realized right away that my bliss wasn't to be. Of the three children with me, the two younger ones were acting too silly for the oldest as soon as we pulled out of the train station. Then one, who hates to eat breakfast, especially Scottish breakfast, became irritable before she finally found food that met with her approval in the Scottish countryside. Another always wandered off unannounced and wanted us to hurry through each castle and museum so that we could move on. The third wanted to spend all her time shopping. There were squabbles about where we should stay and what we should eat, and whining about things not being fair.

Just about the time I was ready to wish I hadn't come and give up the children as hopeless, I decided to take a lesson from the Scots. I'm sure there were always squabbles within each clan as well as between the clans of Scotland, but they were always able to rise above them and show real pride in their clan and their heritage. After trying in vain to change the children, I decided it was time to change myself. I began to think about the good things that had happened. One child had skillfully navigated me through strange roads from the kingdom of Fife to Loch Lomond, with a map and a lot of patience. Another was always wanting to give money to the poor and disabled as well as the street entertainers, and was anxious to carry more than her share of bags when my load looked too heavy. The third was filling me in on English history to match up with the Scottish history we were learning. I started thanking them, telling them how great they were, praising every positive thing I noticed.

I realized once again how easy it is to dwell on the negative and worry about things that are wrong about our children. Recommitting myself to letting these older children know how much I love them and appreciate their many good qualities, I began noticing precious moments I could have missed, including giggling outside the men's room door while listening to our thirteen-year-old sing to his heart's content in an empty bathroom. His song, I think, was a direct result of my praise. The trip became delightful. The more praise I heaped on them, the better they became, and the harder they tried to be better and do better. When they could feel that I really appreciated the little things they had observed, noticed little kindnesses to each other, and praised them for it, it was like I had just traded for new children. They were magnificent.

I went home from that two-day adventure with a firm resolve to get out the family flag and rekindle a love for our family motto, slogan, and scripture, as well as our family songs and traditions, to be more diligent in family prayers, and to develop a real clan spirit for better *and* for worse. Not only that, I decided that the next time I find my three- and five-year-olds not fighting, I'm going to tell them how much I appreciate how nicely they play together, instead of telling them how angry I am when they do fight. Earl Nightingale once said, "Praise to a human being represents what sunlight, water, and soil are to a plant . . . the climate in which one grows best." I have decided to challenge myself to be more positive than negative, to praise instead of prod.

It's a daily struggle to look for good things, to tell children every day that we're proud of them and that there isn't anything they can't do.

Sometimes it means biting your tongue and restraining your urge to talk about a child's annoying idiosyncrasies, especially if she's already aware of them. When asked what one thing in life he would do differently, the Duke of Wellington surprised everyone by referring not to mistakes made in any of his famous battles, but instead simply saying: "I would give more praise."

Sometimes it seems impossible to do, but I am convinced that if we can become skillful at dwelling on the positive and showing our fierce love for our children, not only will they swell with pride and confidence, but it will make a difference in the history of *our* clan!

Surprise Twenty-Six
You Can Change!

When Richard and I were first married, in general, I adored him. However, there were a few things about him that I didn't especially love. But I wasn't worried because I had a plan: I would change him. Yes, indeed, I could easily teach him to be more prompt and notice others' needs. I could hardly wait to spiff up his wardrobe and instruct him on how to look for things that needed to be done around the house and do them immediately. I would teach him to love wedding receptions and other social occasions that he thought were a waste of time.

By the time our first child, Saren, appeared on the scene, on our first anniversary, I had decided that this changing business was not going to be as easy as I had envisioned, at least not with Richard. But now I planned to make this child into my dream child. Starting with a fresh, clean spirit had to be easier! Then child after child arrived, and I began to feel more and more helpless. They were not turning out just exactly as I had planned. Not only that, but when they didn't do things just as I planned, I sometimes became a witch, which I didn't plan at all!

So here I was with a real dilemma. There were so many things I didn't plan: I didn't plan to be ecstatic over a C+ on the report card of a child who had his own way of learning and a tough time in school. Nor did I plan on a child losing his backpack regularly and forgetting all about his major Social Studies Unit. (When his teacher calls to inform me, I pray that she doesn't know we wrote a book called *Teaching Children Responsibility*.)

I didn't plan to have a child who has a major crisis in her life almost every day because she is totally overcommitted and likes it that way. If it isn't reading *David Copperfield* in one night, it's decorating the halls at the high school for the "Battle of the Classes." I try to teach her to simplify, but you see, the juniors *have* to win—so it's floor-to-ceiling zoo, complete with flowers, trees, bars, and of course enormous animals.

I didn't plan to have a five-year-old who is totally demanding of my attention at every waking moment—a need that intensifies in the grocery store when I'm in a hurry or when I'm on the phone. And I didn't figure on having a child who needs less sleep than I do. After years of enforcing bedtimes to a fault, we gave in and allowed her to stay up with the teenagers until 10:00 or 11:00 P.M. Often she even puts *us* to bed.

I didn't plan to produce a perfectionist who vents his frustrations about everything not being perfect (including the weird seeds in the bread) by yelling at me!

I certainly didn't plan to have a husband who is still rarely on time, dresses up when he has to but whose favorite outfit is still purple shorts, an orange T-shirt with holes, and a fluorescent pink Balzac baseball hat from F.A.O. Schwarz. Once in a while he sees something that needs to be fixed, but he figures that if he leaves it long enough, it will fix itself. (I think he doesn't realize that those miraculous "fixings" came from me.) After years of going to wedding receptions by myself, however, he is beginning to go with me once in a while. This happened, funnily enough, just as we could see our own first child's wedding reception on the horizon.

After twenty-six years, I've come to the blinding realization that it is not within my power to change anyone else. Yes, I can influence them and some things change, but a much more important thing to learn is that the one who really needs to change is *me*. I have now learned not to worry about being late for lots of things, and I really like Richard's crazy outfits. I have learned that hiring someone else to fix the broken window is lots simpler than nagging every time he steps in the door. Especially when what he is doing is more important.

Progress means change. The times we grow most are the times when we are required to change, which is especially useful when it is something that we don't like about ourselves. Being a Christian, the word that comes to mind is "repentance." I once heard a Sunday School lesson about repentance that impressed me a great deal. Until then, I often thought of repentance as something I should do when I had committed a grievous sin. It was especially good for robbers and murderers. But on this particular day, the teacher pointed out that repentance simply means to change . . . to change something we don't like about ourselves and replace it with something we would rather be. That meant that it applied to an everyday mother like me—every day.

Spiritually, I have come to believe that the Lord gives us special weaknesses on purpose so that we can not only learn to change, but make those weaknesses our strengths. As I have mentioned, when I became a wife and mother, I think my greatest weakness was impatience. Five years into parenting I was able to discover that our toddler had thrown his shoes, his bottle, and half a bushel of peaches out the back window of our van and actually see the humor in it. I have learned to quit being irate when a teenager misses her curfew, and instead say, "I forgive you for making me worry. What happened?"

Another thing I have become better at changing is self-perceived fears and limitations. There were things that I knew I was pretty good at, but other things that I felt inadequate at and had decided that I couldn't do.

I was a music major in college, specializing in violin. After practicing three hours a day for most of my college years, I realized that I hated performing. I was paralyzed with fear of playing alone and it seemed that my performance days were numbered. But with much encouragement from Richard, I continued. Luckily, I discovered that I loved playing in groups and I decided that it was time to change. I had to use my musical gifts or lose them. At one time when we were living in Washington, D.C., and Richard was director of the President's White House Conference on Parents and Children (and never home), it seemed that the house and the children occupied every waking moment, and I could feel myself burning out. Just about then, I found three wonderful friends (I call them soul sisters) who lived in the area and who just happened to play violin, viola, and cello. Among the four of us, we had twenty-six children and two grandchildren. I decided it was time to change my mind about my feelings about performing. It seemed so wonderful to play together again, and someone suggested that we prepare a concert before I had to move back to the West. That old fear of performing raised its ugly head, but I told myself firmly that I could change, and that it was important to do it.

No one could believe the riotous times we had at rehearsals. If we could have taped the practices, they would have been far funnier than any sitcom on TV. We usually rehearsed with not fewer than seven preschoolers underfoot . . . literally. We learned to practice with our feet on our stands to keep the crawling babies from tipping them over. Our cellist was the president of a large women's organization and dashed in between meetings. The violist had to drive forty-five minutes one way to get there in her teenager's car (which looked a lot like it had just been through the trash masher) in between car pools, teaching viola students, and the frantic schedules of her eight children. Our first violinist had a nursing baby. Though we jokingly tried to convince her to figure out a way to nurse the baby and play the violin at the same time (mothers have to learn to do almost everything else simultaneously), she opted to hum her part while we played and she nursed.

Someone was always late, and there were usually two or three rounds of calls to attend to before we began. But when we finally got rolling, did we have a wonderful time! We loved making beautiful music together. Besides, every rehearsal was such an adventure. About every eight minutes one of the roving pack of little ones needed a Band-Aid, a rescue from a bad dog, a peanut butter sandwich, a clean diaper, or a mediator for negotiations on toys. The upwardly mobile ones danced together while we played, and once even took off all their clothes and had a great romp in the backyard wading pool. The cellist often found my baby hanging on the end pin of her cello, gazing up at her at the end of a movement.

We performed many times together during those few months, and it was always an unbelievable hassle. But the night of our big recital in a large venue in Maryland topped them all, in more ways than one.

One of our members had just returned from a two-week trip to

Hawaii, China, and Egypt, and so we had been practicing ferociously the past two days. The night of the performance she called to ask if I could drive, as she had just realized that the insurance had expired on their car. I had been about to call her to tell her that there was a flat tire on our car and we had no spare. I had been frantically packing as the moving men were arriving the next afternoon, in 90-degree heat with 85 percent humidity as our air conditioning was broken. We decided on the uninsured car.

When we got there (a little later than planned), the other two musicians, who were coming from the other side of the Beltway, had still not arrived. When they did, both were huffing and puffing, red-faced. One explained that her husband had been held up and didn't get home in time to take over with the kids; the other had a van full of cases of grapefruit that her high school kids were selling for a fund-raiser. Somehow the brake had released and the van had coasted across the street and into a neighbor's tree, scattering grapefruit everywhere, not to mention the damage to the car and tree. We all got the giggles about being so "true to the end," and then settled down to the seriousness of the task before us.

I must admit that my eyes filled with tears several times as we played. A tiny wave of fear at the start and at my solo moments was replaced by a true love for the music we were performing and for my beloved friends. As we played a Haydn quartet and Pachelbel's Canon in D, my mind wandered back to all the wonderful times we'd had together, talking and playing and enjoying ourselves. How grateful I was that I had not said, "I have this problem with performing, and besides we're too busy. Let's do it when the kids are grown." How close I had come to not changing, and to missing a great chance to turn my weakness into a strength.

Of course, there are things we would love to do that we do have to give up for our children. Only you can judge when the children are suffering rather than benefitting from a too-strung-out, too-busy mom. In this case, I think our children saw their mothers doing something they loved, and may have learned to love music themselves as they danced.

Yes, the happy news is that not only young mothers, but even we old mothers can change. Not without effort and not every time, but we can do it. Constant change keeps us young and vital, thinking and learning and progressing. More important, we have to realize that we can help those around us, but we really can't plan to change them to make our lives easier. They are who they are. The best chance they have of changing their behavior is to have us change our reaction to it.

One of the most glorious things about being a mother is the potential for personal growth. As we change, we realize that "We don't see things as they are, we see things as we are" (as Anaïs Nin says). Your idiosyncratic husband and engaging children force you to change and sometimes see life a little differently. The only problem is, the need to change never ends. There's still so much of it to do!

Surprise Twenty-Seven
You Must Watch for the Moments, Because Tomorrow They'll Be Gone

I had not seen him for two years—Uncle Cyril, my dad's closest brother, once so vigorous and agile, now in the grasp of time at ninety years. The same smile was there that I remembered as a child, but more wrinkled; same skin but so transparent; same body but stiff, shrinking, fragile; and most especially the same clear, sharp mind and dry wit.

For an hour, in a living room filled with memorabilia—wedding pictures, portraits and snapshots of children and grandchildren—we talked. Uncle Cyril even played two or three shaky but familiar old songs on his little organ and puffed out a favorite hymn on his harmonica before he became exhausted and gasped for breath.

Soon he regained his composure and we talked about his childhood, especially things that he could remember about his parents, who are my grandparents. We talked about his life as a child with my dad.

Just being in his house brought memories gushing back of my own life as a child and the romps I had with his children, my cousins, and the good food Aunt Gladys prepared for us there. Precious memories of my own dad, already ten years gone (and so much like this wonderful man), filled my mind, and I was a little girl again.

After bidding a fond farewell, which I knew might be my last, I walked effortlessly to the car in a body that I was now so much more grateful for. During the half-hour trip home, I started wondering what memories my children would have of me when I am ninety . . . when all the days of perpetual picking up and practicing, arguing about whether or not to have breakfast cereal for lunch and dinner, are over.

Will my children remember my irritation at a three-year-old's messes or my tantrums when a child loses his orthodontic neckgear . . . again, or will they remember reading stories and occasional tennis matches?

Which will they remember best: Feeling angry with me for sending them to the repenting bench, or laughing at my hopeless efforts (complete with life-threatening spills) to drop a ski and slalom behind our little water-ski boat?

Which will they remember hearing most: "Practice! . . . Be sure to be in by midnight! . . . Get in the car, we're late!" or, "I love you more than you'll ever know," and, "There isn't anything you can't do!"

Will they remember me always rushing off to meet the next deadline (which usually involved getting another child someplace) or will they remember our long bedroom talks after midnight?

Still deep in thought, I pulled up in front of our little summer lakeside cabin, slipped inside unnoticed and began fixing a casserole for dinner. Before five minutes had passed, Talmadge came and put his hand on my shoulder and said, "Mom, come out to raft with us. It's so hot and the water is so cool! You can watch me dive!"

"You go ahead and I'll come down when I get this in the oven."

"Oh, Mom, c'mon," was his response. "You always say that, but you hardly ever make it to the water."

Suddenly coming to my senses, I looked at Talmadge, gazed into those pleading eyes—only ten years, five months, and twenty-one days old for a single day—and said, "Let's have toast and jam for dinner. I simply can't wait to see you dive!"

Ah, how often we miss those moments! We are so occupied with the busyness of our lives that we just don't notice them. I doubt if Talmadge remembered that moment that past summer, but I still do. If we're honest with ourselves, we must admit that often when we kill ourselves to get to a recital or a play or a baseball game, thinking we are doing the kid a great favor, the child is glad to have us there, but it is we who benefit most from seeing our yesterday's baby play a solo or hit a home run. There is so much talk about being there for the child and so little about being there for *us*. An old Arabian proverb says: "Four things come not back—the spoken word, the sped arrow, the past life, and the neglected opportunity."

When we begin our journey in life with husband and children, we expect that our days, months, and years will be filled with joy and happiness. As we get down the road a bit, we realize that our days are filled with one crisis after another. The pressure to juggle all the balls in our life becomes overwhelming and we feel more like we are surviving than really living. It's the old "gerbil on the treadmill" again. Henry Thoreau said, "It's not enough to be busy; so are the ants. The question is, what are we busy about?" So often we think, "After I get this project done, after this dinner, after the school carnival, after this deal is closed . . . I can start enjoying life."

I must admit that I still struggle with that mentality. However, I have discovered something that truly does make life exciting. I have realized that real joy does not come in years, or months, or even days. It comes in moments. The most interesting part is that those moments are always there if we're looking for them. They may come in the form of a beautiful sunset. Or a child who leaves a little note on your pillow thanking you for helping him with his homework. Spontaneous surprises, funny faces, massive mistakes, cute comments, inspirational ideas, breathtaking beauty, generous gratitude, and happy hugs all come in moments.

Our lives are full of wonderful moments if we just watch for them. Elizabeth Barrett Browning wrote, "Earth's crammed with heaven / And every common bush afire with God; / But only he who takes off his shoes, / The rest of us sit around and pluck blackberries."

I challenge you to really watch for your moments. I promise that they're there if you're watching for them and they're forever gone if you aren't. Richard and I call them "serendipities," which is defined as something good that happens while you are looking for something else . . . a happy accident. For one week, write down the "moments" from your day. You'll be amazed at how much fun you're having!

One of my all-time favorite moments came on a day when I thought I certainly wasn't having very much fun. I had finally squeezed in time for an early morning aerobics class with two preschoolers in tow. This was not just any preschoolers; it was Eli when he was almost five and Charity, who was just about two. Eli, a born tease, was generally the bane of Charity's existence, as he was still trying to make her pay for taking over his place as the baby of the family. Every day he thought of new ways to make her scream, ranging from taking her toys to sitting on her face. And she had developed the most marvelous scream, sure to demand immediate attention.

On this particular morning I was completely exasperated by the end of the class. Charity and Eli had been underfoot and fussing the whole hour. (I was praying that nobody knew I had written a book called *Teaching Your Children Joy*.) Suddenly realizing that I was late for my next meeting, I gathered up my mat and papers and dashed to the parking lot. It was a cold winter morning and the parking lot was sheer ice. As I approached the van with arms loaded, I realized that Eli and Charity were not with me. I looked back and saw cute Eli with one arm firmly wrapped around Charity's shoulder and the other hand holding her chubby little hand, carefully negotiating her across the icy parking lot.

It crossed my mind that he would probably find a snowbank and throw her into it before he reached me, but he didn't. Soon he was directly under me, still with his little sister tucked under his arm. He looked directly up at me like he was gazing at the Empire State Building, and with his great big, adorable, toothless grin, he waited for just a moment with that little smile frozen on his face, then said, "Don't you wish you had a camera?" That was a moment!

Those "longer moments" called family trips and vacations are important, too, but it's the wrong approach to think that you have just two weeks once a year to enjoy your family, and then you take a deep breath and hold it while you suffer through the other eleven months and two weeks. I can almost guarantee that no matter how stressed you feel or what the pressures are in your life, if you take the time to look for those moments, they'll be there all the time, and you'll be enjoying life . . . one moment at a time.

Because I can also guarantee that tomorrow you'll be old and they'll be gone.

Surprise Twenty-Eight
What a Difference Five Years Makes

It had been an exhausting day, filled with "blood, sweat, and tears" as usual . . . one crisis after another. Late the night before, I had spent hours comforting a seventeen-year-old who felt dejected because she had "no real friends," hadn't been asked to the Junior Prom, *and* was unable to run the world as she thought it should be run.

That morning our sensitive sixteen-year-old needed to be reassured once again that even though she was sure of it this time, she probably did *not* have cancer. Every day recently, she had been sure that she had a new form of cancer . . . cancer of the elbow or cancer of the eyelash. After profuse reassurances, I convinced her that she was probably okay for another day. This totally fussy eater then promptly proceeded to turn down every option for breakfast but toast. I warned her that someday she was going to have to broaden her tolerance for food a little and learn to eat something besides bread, broccoli, and licorice.

And our fourteen-year-old was having a difficult time opening the door to his room for all the junk inside. He was struggling for good grades and was wondering how he could have been sent to such a weird family.

I was late for a dentist appointment because our demanding baby needed to be changed and had a tantrum because she couldn't wear her Halloween costume in May.

"Please tell me this gets easier," I pleaded with the parents of some almost-grown children sitting next to me at a dinner that evening. They looked at each other, smiled, and in unison shook their heads. "No, it just gets to be a different kind of hard."

I clenched my teeth and braced myself for the next five years. I felt like an airline pilot whose landing gear didn't work, going in for a crash landing. I didn't know if I could survive!

Now . . . years down the road, in retrospect, though every family has different challenges at different times, I am here to offer hope. It *is* getting easier . . . and incredibly rewarding. The baby has grown from being a demanding, spoiled, dependent toddler who was driving us crazy to a demanding, spoiled, adorable first grader who does everything for herself.

Oh yes, we still have several crises each day—a high school senior who has too many fingers in too many pies and a ten-year-old who is a professional worrier and can't control his temper. We still have ten basketball teams in the winter and mounds of laundry and "eating machines" to deal with, but it *is* getting easier!

I have discovered that there is no greater joy than seeing your children become young adults who are broadening themselves and actually contributing—not only to the family but to society! Five years later, here are the same problem children, revisited:

Our fourteen-year-old, who never communicated verbally very much, is now nineteen, six feet five, 190 pounds, and studying abroad in Israel, preparing to leave for a voluntary church assignment in England. His letters make us realize that we're just beginning to know him. Shortly after his arrival in Jerusalem on his nineteenth birthday, he wrote:

Today we went to the Temple Mount and the Dome of the Rock and the Wailing Wall and got some great pictures. It was amazing! On our way out of the city we saw some Arab kids playing soccer so we went over and started talking to them. We made them really happy just sitting there talking to them for half an hour. It made us feel good, too! On our way back to the center we walked by the Garden of Gethsemane and in the old city we walked along the Via De Larosa [Via Dolorosa], which is the path where Christ carried the cross. What a great birthday! I *am* a little homesick but being away from home makes me realize that I live in the *best* country, best state, best city, and best family in the whole world!

Love,
Josh

Our whining sixteen-year-old picky eater is now twenty-one and doing humanitarian service and missionary work in Romania. She writes:

Yesterday we ate lunch at a darling lady's who had sacrificed time and money to provide a meal for us. We had rolls with carp egg spread and soup for an appetizer with huge chunks of pork fat with some bristles of hair still sticking out of it. Because she had been saving money all week to be able to provide this meal for us, I ate most of it in awe of myself. Just as I thought I was at the end of my ordeal, our darling hostess brought out these plates of intestine sausage filled with everything you can imagine from a pig, but luckily there were mashed potatoes to help get it down. The other day a different family served us rabbit and then graciously showed us a little statue of a rabbit and pointed to the parts we had eaten. At church I'm teaching people how to eat balanced meals—that drinking water will not make them fat, and that pure pork fat gristle isn't really very high in nutrients.

Sometimes there are moments of pure joy. The other day we saw three of the ladies we've been working with coming down the street in the distance—these three beautiful women glowing with happiness were walking along the street with their little four-year-old Alexander, with sun shining through their hair. It was so beautiful. They've made such progress. I don't think I've ever been that purely happy before. I couldn't stop smiling the whole day.

Love,
Shawni

P.S. I think I have cancer in my left foot.

Our seventeen-year-old was now twenty-two. She went off to college, became her house president at Wellesley College, and *did* run her own little world for a while. She was surrounded by myriads of outstanding friends from all over the world, and is now doing humanitarian service and missionary work in Bulgaria.

She writes:

I love the orphanages. The babies with birth defects need so much love and have so little. They sit in their dirty little cribs all their lives with only cockroaches to play with. I love to hold them close and play music to them and see their heads move in time to the music. I love the beautiful little girl with the misshaped head due to an inoperable brain tumor who clings to me, the little boy who's so stiff and sweaty and smiles in surprise at my touch, the baby with the huge blue eyes and useless little paralyzed legs who loves music. They all love to be held and light up at a gentle touch after initial shock and fear. I want them to know that someone loves them and that sometime in their short lives someone held them close and made them feel like a precious real person and maybe someday if I'm really, really good I can be friends with those precious spirits in Heaven.

Love,
Saren

What a difference five years can make! Who knows . . . in another five years we may not be so lucky. But for now, be encouraged. Know that at least for most children, there will be moments in your family history that make your struggles and worries and the feeling that you'd like to pull your hair out worth it! Hang on—there's a light at the end of the tunnel!

Surprise Twenty-Nine
To Succeed in Your Career as a Mother, You Need a Plan

(Note: Saren says this chapter is boring. But for desperate mothers who feel out of whack, I think it is the most valuable.)

In talking to mothers from all walks of life all across America in seminars and radio and TV talk shows, as well as just one on one, I discovered something interesting. One night when mother after mother called in on a TV talk show with problems, I realized that most women who are unhappy when they are home with their children—whether they work outside the home or not—feel that way because they lack the "tools" of their profession.

Let's face it. Happy homes and good children don't usually just happen, any more than a good company with great expectations just happens to become a Fortune 500 company. I've always said that the complexities of creating a happy family are just as difficult and much more important than being the president or CEO of a large corporation.

Let's look at the career of mothering strictly from a business viewpoint for a moment. First of all, we know how scary the first day of a new job can be. Most of us can relate to the uneasy feeling of not knowing exactly what is expected of us or how this new job will fit in with our lives. Maybe co-workers didn't like the person who had this job last, or maybe they liked her so much that it's going to be hard to fill her shoes. These feelings are not unlike those we feel when handed that first new baby to take home and "raise." We wonder if we're up to this new, life-changing job. Maybe your own mother was not a good example and you're determined to do better, but you just don't know how. Or maybe you felt that your mother was so good that you fear you'll never measure up.

As our goals for progress in our new job and our list of expectations for ourselves and others are defined, we begin to use these goals to help us accomplish the job. We become more and more comfortable, and the more we use these tools and fine-tune them to make things work better, the more we enjoy the job. That stimulates us to make even more plans to improve our performance. Things don't always turn out as planned, but if we have a goal in mind and are always thinking about how to make things better, and doggedly work at it, eventually things do start working.

Remember that the key to success in any job is to love it. You may not love every minute of every day, but I agree with Sister Mary Laruetta, who said, "To be successful, the first thing you have to do is fall in love with your work." Keep remembering in all your planning that there is no greater work than that of being a mother.

It's hard to love an assembly-line job! Creativity, long-range planning, systems that work out problems afford the challenging and rewarding jobs. But a job that makes a real contribution to society is the best of all.

Every mother has multiple careers. Their other careers might include anything from the president of a large company to church worker, community leader, part-time teacher, or PTA president. In dealing with these complications, we need to focus on a regular basis on the fact that our *family* is our first priority. This makes mothering and taking care of our spouses our most important career. C. S. Lewis said it straightforwardly: "Homemaking is surely in reality the most important work in the world. What do ships, railways, mine cars and government exist for except that people may be safe in their own home? The homemaker's is the job for which all others exist."

We could also look at our children as fledgling "spin-off" companies . . . each struggling to get a good start. As chairman of the board, we have to fight to help them reach their potential, even though we don't know exactly what that new company will become or the far-reaching effect it will have on others. New companies are always difficult to manage and never succeed without bumps and struggles. Clear goals, careful planning, hundreds of hours of work and guidance, a vision of possibilities, and the tenacity to make it happen are the right tools for these fledglings. Every hour invested with a child while he/she is young and impressionable is like an investment in pure gold. The returns are vast and immeasurable.

All this sounds great, but let's be realistic. You may well be asking yourself, "How can I really do this? How can I change things when I feel that I'm just barely surviving as it is? I'm hanging on for all I'm worth, but I'm losing my grip!" If you're anything like I am, you will need to call a "time out" in this process of mothering. Richard and I often ask people to turn old clichés around. For this one, you need to quit saying to yourself, "Don't just sit there; do something," and say, instead, "Don't just do something; sit there"—sit there and *think* about your family and its needs.

Whether you are just beginning your career as a mother or are about to burn out, I'm challenging you first to get way for a whole twenty-four hours. You may gasp and say, "That is impossible," but think again. Solicit the aid of your husband, mother, sister, or a friend or neighbor to help you. I usually go to a motel where it is quiet and I can lock myself away from the world. It is such an amazing experience to lay a pen on the desk, walk into the bathroom, come back out, and find it *still there!* You'll love it.

I've also tried choosing a beautiful spot outdoors and working in the car when I could only find a few hours. Another great place to think is the public library. Find a corner where no one will recognize you and want to talk, and plan away. I like to do this about once every six months, but you need to adjust according to your own needs. Whether it's a few hours in your car, a couple in the library or two days locked in a hotel room ordering room service while you consider your life and revamp some things that aren't working, I can almost guarantee that you'll feel better about your life.

Below is a list of things that I've done in what I call "My Day Away." Again, these are only ideas for you to use to help you think of your own. It's such a marvelous time to take inventory of your life. I didn't do all these things at once; the list consists of all the things that I have tried over the years, so don't be overwhelmed. Each takes mental energy, not only to create but to implement as you think about what you want and how to achieve it.

1. Write a statement of your purpose as a mother—a "mission statement," if you will. What do you really want to accomplish in your career as a mother? Think about this career to its fullest extension. Remember, mothering never ends; it just gets bigger. Your career deserves some vision and plans for implementation.

2. Think about your long-range goals for *you* for your lifetime. Write down what you need physically, emotionally, socially, mentally, and spiritually to accomplish those goals.

3. Establish that there are "seasons" in your life: spring (your youth and college days); summer (the childbearing and child-rearing years); fall (for me, a time when I can be more heavily involved in a career or activities outside the home); and winter (a time to enjoy getting older, traveling, grandchildren, etc.). Determine to spend most of your time and energy on the season you are in right now, but look forward to the other seasons as well. This is an exercise in casting your mind over your life as a whole.

4. Set some medium-range goals for what you wish to be like five years from now. What personality traits would you like to possess and amplify by then? Think of how old each child will be and what kind of relationship you'd like to have with them five years from now.

5. If you are married, set some goals to be a better partner to your husband. Remember that admiration and appreciation are the keys to letting your husband know that you love him. So often we let the traits that we don't admire and appreciate get in the way of the traits that we do. Write down a list of things you admire about your husband, and specific actions you can do to show your admiration and appreciation. Determine to sit down with

him when you get home and commit to working together as a partnership in more concrete ways. (Two suggestions might be having a date once a week, and a planning session on Sunday nights where you talk not only about the week's activities but also what you can do to help each other.) You might decide to have what Richard and I call a "Five-Facet Review" each month. This consists of going out to dinner and talking about each of the children's needs; physically, emotionally, socially, mentally, and spiritually. We take notes on little things we can each do to help. It is an excellent way to keep tabs on your rapidly growing children and also to spot small problems and do something about them before they get out of hand.

6. Consciously take time to survey each child's progress. Think about his/her interests and gifts, and what you are doing to help magnify them. I actually keep a journal on each child and use this time away to write down things that have happened since the last entry, including the wise and wonderful things they have said. I record my observations of what each child is like and what I appreciate about him/her at each age. This little book is my college graduation or wedding gift to them (whichever comes first).

7. Decide to quit spending so much time "keeping score." Don't worry as much about whether or not your child gets better grades or plays a musical instrument or is "popular" as you worry about whether or not he (or she) is really being educated, what you can do to improve the qualify of his life, and how sensitive he is toward others. Try to worry more about your relationship with your husband and children and "enjoying the journey" than you do about "getting there."

8. Determine to set family goals. After you have thought of some suggestions, let your "fledglings" help you formulate them. If you are married, start by drafting these goals as a partnership. If you are single, working on goals with your little fledglings is a sure way to glue your family together. Almost nothing works better than working on common goals.

You might want to have a family "major" and "minor" for the

year. We have used everything from learning a foreign language together to making new friends as our points of focus. The possibilities are limitless. Another good glue for a family is family traditions. Think about some fun new traditions that you can all look forward to.*

9. Most importantly, remember that mothering is *hard!* Expect mistakes and failures. That's what progress is all about. Learn from your boo-boos, and apologize to your family for the times you judged too harshly or became a witch and cackled over "Herman" when he fell over the bike you told him to put away forty times. Write down your plans to become more patient, more understanding, more loving.

After you've completed all this hard mental work, don't forget to allow some time for yourself . . . whether you decide to do *nothing* or do something you've always wanted like watch the news or read the paper without interruptions. Or just forget the world and relax in the tub.

On your way home, visualize yourself as being involved in the world's most exciting career. You are shaping lives, breeding self-confidence, discovering talent, directing these little people toward making contributions, and improving yourself as you do. You are doing your part in a grass-roots way to strengthen the crumbling American family unit, which forms the true basis of our society.

When you get home, your family may find that you have taken off your witch hat and put away your broom. I get much nicer while I'm gone. This precious time sprinkles me with Tinkerbell's fairy dust and suddenly I can put a lot of things into perspective. Richard seems so wonderful . . . especially if he is the one who has been holding down the fort! (Actually, I look pretty good to him about then, too.) The children have gotten so much cuter while I was gone, and it is exciting to go on with life.

*If you need ideas, see *Three Steps to a Strong Family,* a book Richard and I wrote together (New York: Simon & Schuster, 1994), now available in paperback (1995). In fact, if you feel you need concrete tools to teach your child joy, responsibility, sensitivity, and values, check for our books under each of these titles, (*Teaching* . . .), all published by Simon & Schuster.

Most of any success I've had as a mother I owe first to prayer and next to these "saw-sharpening" sessions. I plead for guidance from heaven even longer and harder than usual . . . as though I'm totally relying on the Lord for the success of my family. Then I have to think and work as though it all depends on me. Some goals I work on diligently. With others, I am amazed when they come to pass, often through inspiration, even though I haven't done much to make them happen consciously. In some cases, when I go back a year later to see what I wrote, I find many of the things I have accomplished—right there on my list. The mind is a wonderful machine. Once goals have been registered there and visualized as coming to pass, they often happen by remote control.

If you spend a little time each year working out yearly goals, each month on monthly goals, and each week on things that need to happen on a day-to-day basis, you will be astonished at how many of these lifetime goals do actually come to pass.

So, mothers, unite! Don't allow yourself to think of your career as merely an assembly line job—cooking and cleaning, chauffeuring and servicing. Take your career as a mother seriously. Take the time to think and plan, struggle and strain, be creative and constant. Use planning tools, and remember that your career takes dedication and determination, prayer and persistence, talent and tenacity, madness and mental energy, humor and sensitivity—and lot of overtime.

Yet its impact is staggering. Good mothering can change the world at a grass-roots level. Instead of filling the business of raising children with busyness, use vision and planning tools to fill it with success!

Surprise Thirty
Mothering Is Harder Than You Can Imagine and More Joyful Than You Can Fathom

For two weeks in 1994, we had been watching the magnificent showmanship of the Winter Olympics at Lillehammer, in Norway. Tears spilled out of my eyes as I watched the magic of the moment when Dan Jansen, after finally winning his long-coveted Gold Medal, made his victory lap around the crammed ice arena. Clutching his darling baby and a bundle of tulips in one arm, he waved to the ecstatic crowd with the other. Ten long, grueling years of tenacity had finally paid off, and his face communicated his joy, exhilaration, and relief.

It was the year when we were pulling for Nancy Kerrigan and trying to feel sorry for silly Tonya Harding. We were thrilled by the five Gold medals for Bonnie Blair and we triumphed with the Norwegian champion, Koss. I was almost overcome by grief for the skiers and skaters whose names I have already forgotten as they experienced freak accidents or one tiny misstep or slight miscalculation that instantly left the dreams they had pursued for twelve hours a day, year after year, in ashes. For some, it was the end. For most, it was a stark disappointment but also an incentive to do better in four years. Because of their failures, they were compelled to go on.

One night, after watching the inevitable triumphs and tragedies, I lay in bed trying to go to sleep but couldn't because I was worried about one of our kids. It occurred to me how much being a mother is like being an Olympian. The deadline may not be as clear, but the discipline may require even more persistence and optimism, and certainly requires longer hours.

There are days full of frustration and disappointment and times when we feel that every muscle aches and our emotion is stretched to capacity. As I thrashed about, I calculated that I had spent the last twenty-four years parenting. I thought back to just the last twenty-four hours. At the crack of dawn, as I folded clothes and threw yesterday's batch of wash in the dryer, I realized that our high school junior had slept through his alarm as he had been up until 1:00 A.M. trying, with my help, to figure what on earth Walt Whitman, Robert Frost, and Emily Dickinson meant when they wrote certain poems. He had missed his early morning class and still needed help with e.e. cummings before he went to school.

Our sixteen-year-old was frantic about Pep Club tryouts that day and her campaign for the School Senate on Friday. We had helped her prepare posters for the walls and hundreds of badges to pass out at school. This little project we had finished by about 2:30 A.M.

By 7:30 A.M., our thirteen-year-old was begging for help on a math assignment. Luckily I remembered absolutely nothing about algebra, so I told him if he wanted my help, he was going to have to practice the piano. I knew that would get him off my back.

Our eleven-year-old had a big oral report to do on England at nine forty-five: we scrambled to get the last few visual aids rounded up and his note cards organized. "Since we've lived in England," he said, "I think she expects a really great report." That made me feel better! "Oh, plus did I tell you that we are supposed to bring a little tasty treat for everyone so they can sample British food?" he added sheepishly.

Our nine-year-old was trying to learn a new piano piece and needed my help. At least he would accept help. The seven-year-old, who is an absolute perfectionist with a flaming temper, screams almost every minute of his practice time because he can't get something just perfect immediately, then he gets mad at *me* when he can't get it right.

By now the high school and junior high kids had gotten themselves out the door after a hasty breakfast and a quick "huddle" (prayer) at the door. The elementary kids were arguing with me about whether or not it would be important to wear a sweatshirt that day as they were sure that it was already 47 degrees outside, and we dashed out just in time to stop by the grocery store on the way to get an "English treat."

I came home feeling bad that we had missed our morning family meeting and the garbagemen . . . and pretty burned out as I saw the breakfast remains and the leftover scraps from the campaign posters and forgotten lunches. Not only that, I knew my day had barely begun as I needed to pick up invitations and other supplies at the Boy Scout Center for our third son's Eagle Scout Court of Honor the following night, get flowers for a hopeful Pep Clubber, get groceries and organize dinner, as well as bake a cake for a birthday party at the homeless shelter that we were helping with that night. Four of our children would be participating. And I needed to get a package in the mail to our two daughters attending college in Boston and fill them in on all the latest family news.

For a moment my thoughts flashed back to the daily struggles of the Olympians. Yes, there are similarities. Except that when you have a victory as a mother, there are no screaming crowds, no cascading flowers or reams of telegrams. But there are Gold, Silver, and Bronze medals. They're not presented to the strains of the national anthem as you wave and beam from the podium; instead, they come in quiet moments.

Sometimes they are just little moments, like the day our seven-year-old bundle of perfection came to me a few hours after he had been naughty and we had worked out a fair punishment. He hugged my leg with tremendous sincerity and solemnly vowed with a toothless grin, "Mom, if I had my choice between you and Michael Jordan's wife for a mother, I would *still* choose you." (I think he had seriously considered the other option.)

My thoughts flashed back to the hug I got last night from our six feet five, 200-pound seventeen-year-old, who said, "Thanks for the nice dinner, Mom . . . especially the brownie cake," and the way our fourteen-year-old always says, "'Bye, I love you," when she talks to me on the phone, even if she has a friend standing right by her.

After the summer we spent in Japan with all nine children, I found a note under my pillow the day we got home from our thoughtful eighteen-year-old, expressing her sincere thanks for the trip and telling me how brave she thought I was!

Wonderful expressions of gratitude are the real medals of mothering. Saren, our oldest, inherited her dad's ability to write poetry. The following "Gold Medal" was presented to me on my birthday just before she graduated from high school:

I remember
Watching the cracks in the ceiling move,
Laying on the waterbed,
So sick with some forgotten malady.
And I was so small.

But you were there.

I fell off my bike,
Smacked my head,
Raked my skin on the cruel gravel.

But you were there.

I felt discouraged,
Dejected, alone . . . but still

You were there.

I came home late and got up late
I argued with everything you said
I missed the bus
I hardly said thanks

But always and forever,
You were there.

And this one was sent home from college at Wellesley in 1990:

When the echoes close in
And no one will absorb my heart,
The little girl with messy hair

And a purple leotard
That lives deep inside,
Runs barefoot through forests
And flowers to arms that are
Always open
And Love
That spans all miles.
Love,
Saren

There is no greater joy in life than that of being a mother. Along with the job description comes not only chauffeur, cook, maid, and drill sergeant, but most importantly, gardener of souls—fertilizer, weeder, waterer, exposer to the light, and then watcher as each seedling grows and becomes it own beautiful self.

The most momentous event since the birth of our first baby has just occurred in our family: Our First Marriage. The dust has just settled, and all the massive preparations and calculations of *when*, *where*, and *how* for wedding dresses and cakes, ivy wreaths, bridesmaid's dresses, groomsmen's tuxedos, and flower arrangements have passed. Hundreds of hours have been spent choosing and dealing with caterers, photographers, and video guys, doing everything just as Shawni has always dreamed of for her perfect wedding (within the boundaries of a certain budget). What we have left is a wonderful new son-in-law. At last, I have ten children!

We also have a sensational new daughter, because she is now also a wife. She and Dave are setting out to make their own family unit. This beautiful, sensitive daughter has experienced the world in many ways . . . from growing up in a semi-crazy family who have lived all over the world to attending Boston University and doing eighteen months of humanitarian service and missionary work in Romania. She and her husband will graduate from BYU after one more semester and will be off to some unknown place next year at this time. One thing she does know, however, is that she soon wants to fulfill the dream that has been foremost in her mind since the first day her baby brother was placed in her arms when she was a tiny two-year-old. *She wants to be a mother!*

I'll have to be honest and tell her the whole truth about mothering. It's a risk. A big one. You never know what you'll get. But as Erica Jong says, "The trouble is, if you don't risk everything, you risk even more." You risk missing the most amazing experiences of your life!

When she asks me what to expect, I'll tell her to expect surprises. I'll tell her that mothering is the hardest thing she will ever do, but that it is also much more joyful than even she, who has longed to be a mother for so many years, can fathom.

It has been hard for Shawni to think about leaving our family and starting out with a new partner. But I reminded her about the birds' nest in our charcoaler this spring. One day we noticed a mother bird busily building a big soft nest through the hole in the back of our charcoal grill. Every day we watched her carefully build, one straw at a time, then lay eggs, then pop in with long worms dangling from her mouth as the little blue eggs cracked open to reveal chicks with huge yellow mouths, shooting wide to be fed every time we carefully lifted the lid to sneak a peek. Before we knew it, the little birds were hopping around inside. They were so exciting to watch. One day, they were ready to fly. We were apprehensive for both mother and babies as we watched them struggle and flop again and again—and then finally fly.

All that mother bird's time for weeks had been spent caring for those babies, feeding them and protecting them for this moment when they would launch themselves into the real world. This mother would never know if her tedious efforts were worth it until she saw them fly. And so it is with the monumental task of motherhood: The real test comes when the babies fly. We may have a pang of sorrow, but it is soon replaced with joy as we watch our babies spread their wings and accomplish our goal . . . to work ourselves out of a job and see them ride the wind. Shawni's beaming face and love for Dave, for her family, for people, and for life tells me that it's going to be a fun ride—inevitable disasters and all!

No, nothing, not even the Olympics, can touch the trials or the rewards of being a mother, where the bottom line is not winning the game or having huge financial success, but giving unconditional love and making a success of human lives. Truly, motherhood, complete with its valley depths and mountain peaks, is life's most astounding experience!

Postscript: Poetry
and Letters to Die For

✦

By now, probably many of you are saying, "I could have written this book. My experiences have been different, but strangely the same. And oh, the stories *I* have lived!" And I would say, "You're right. Do it! Do it for yourself, and for the rest of us, and especially for your children. They will want to know." True, there are days when it feels as though the world is crashing in on top of you, but there *are* those magnificent moments.

As I close this book, I'd like to share a few of those moments in order to show you why I love being a mother so much. Even though I am still a pretty consistent witch and struggle with expending volumes of time and energy keeping up with the kids, there are those "paydays" when you get your reward. I'm including some things that provided some of my best paydays . . . poetry and letters to die for. Usually they came on Mother's Day or my birthday, when Richard required a poem for me from each child as he composed one himself. Some are just funny letters that I received along the way that made me laugh and realize that kids are worth all the trouble.

I am grateful that the kids didn't reveal my worst witch moments. Children are so forgiving! As Emma Goldman has said, "No one has yet fully realized the wealth of sympathy, kindness, and generosity hidden in the soul of a child."

Again, I'm sure you have or will have some of these in your own file. Save them when they come, and treasure them. They are your gold medals.

The following poems were presented to me on my forty-first birthday. (The spelling has been left intact.)

Mother's Touch

The child murmurs softly,
Crying quietly of his troubles
The day has been cold and bitter
And the echoes of painful scowls and cruel laghter
Run edlessly through his head
And feel to him like pounding thunder

The tender touch of mother

The peaceful, pleasant feelings,
And the sweet soothing voice,
"Hush," she whispers,
And her voice sounds like velvet.

The child's contented figure stirs quietly,
Wrapped in the wrmth of his mother's touch.

—Shawni [16]

My Mother's Sweet Smile

My mother can tell me so much in her face,
Her cheerful smiling mouth can tell me the case.
She shows me she's happy, worried or sad,
Angry, excited or extremely glad.
She shows me I'm special, that there's no one like me
That I can be someone and that I am free.
I watch her smile stand in crowded places.
And I'm glad she's my mom, seeing all the dull faces

With her sweet sensitive smile, she says,
  "I love you"
I proudly smile back, for I love her too.

—Saydi [12]

You are like a big blue sky and a bright sun to lite up many lives or help us. And you are like a teacher at home and not at school. You make life much easier. And you are very beautiful. I love you, I hope you're feeling better.

—Love, from Jonah [10]

You are like a butuful spontaneous
horse that always has to work
for her babies.

You are sophisticated and
sensitive.
You have the sweetest smile.

—Love, Talmadge [8]

I love you

Mom, you are
Sweet as candy
Pretty as a flower
Soft as a cushion
Nice as Santa
And pretty as a girlfriend.

HAPPY BIRTHDAY, MOM!

—Noah [7]

Here is a short note from Josh (who was always brief when he was a child). He gave it to me the day after I helped his third-grade class with a science project.

Dear Mom,
Thank you for getting the eye balls for us. We couldn't have
done it without you. Thank you for going so far out to get them.
Love, Josh. [9]

Here is a birthday poem from eleven-year-old Eli when he was obsessed with rhyming:

I LOVE YOU WITH ALL OF MY HEART.

FOR THIS REASON I HOPE WE WILL NEVER PART.

YOU ARE THE BEST IN THE WEST

YOU ARE NEVER EVEN A PEST *[this is not what he claims during the week]*

I LOVE YOU SO

I HOPE YOU NEVER LOSE A TOE.

I LOVE YOU SO MUCH

YOUR FOOD TASTES JUST LIKE DUTCH.

I LOVE YOU

MARACULASSLY AWESOME

OH MY LAWSOME SHE'S BEAUTIFUL

MY MOM!!!!!!!!!!!!!!

A valentine letter from Saydi at seven:

Dear Mother,
   I really think that you are terrific and pretty even thoug you
are fat and I know that is just that your pregnant. I love you very
much. I like the way you take care of me when I am sick or sad
or even mad. I am so glad that I came onto this earth with my
family. I really do appreciate your doing all that stuff for me and
all my brothers and sisters and my dad. I can't wait to have a
new baby in my room. I really think your cooking is great. Do
you know what else? I think you have a lot of talents. They are
singing, playing the piano and violin too. I dont think it was such
a good idea about you being fat.

                                        Love Saydria Joy Eyre

A poem from Saren at thirteen:

A Mother Is . . .

A mother is the sun
Opening flowers,
Bringing new life.
She feels like a warm
Spring day.
She is a wolf and
A gentle lamb, in one.
She feels the feelings
Of her children
Deep within her.
She crys,
She laughs.
She is delicate yet
Steady, firm.
She's a day at its fullest,
Sun straight overhead.
This is how a mother should be.
My mother is this way.
I LOVE HER.

From Talmadge in the fourth grade:

Dear Mom,
    Mom, I love you. You are nice. If I could give you anything in
the world it would be two weeks off of me and all of us.

Love, Talmadge, [11]

On one birthday I found these notes from Noah, two and a half, Talmadge, four, and Eli, five months (with a little help from his dad):

Dear Mudder,
    I like you a lot. You are my funny mudder. [Noah]

Dear Mom,
    I think you're cute. I love you. I hope you like these flowers
from us. [Talmadge]
Dear Mother,
    I only spit on those I love. [Eli]

A voluminous writer, here is a little note that Charity, eight, composed for me in school one day:

Mom,
    You smell as a flower! You are as pretty as a flower! BUT you
are more nice and sweet and much more understanding. Another thout [thought] you smeel much better than a flower! You
are much prettyer than a flower. You are wonderful.
I love you.

As a senior who had just graduated from high school, Shawni wrote:

Dear Mom,
    Ever since I was young, being with you has always given me a
special warm feeling inside. You have taught me most of what I
know and I've always lived with you comforted by knowing you
were always going to be there for me. I love it when people say
we look alike and that you used to be like me when you were
younger, because it gives me hope that maybe someday I'll grow
up and be less shy and be like you.
    Mom, one of the things that makes me so reluctant to go away
to college next year is that I'll miss you so much. I just have an
empty place in my heart when I'm away from you.
    Thanks especially for helping with my college decision because
I know you care so much about it. Thanks for accepting me for
who I am and being patient with my weird personality. No matter
what happens next year, let's always be best friends. I love you.

In the fifth grade, Eli was given an assignment to write an essay entitled "My Dream":

My dream is to become a student at Harvard and get a masters degree and then go play in the NBA. I would love to have this career because I would be a good student in school and maybe a famous Basketball player. If I was, I would be very greatful. With some of the money i get i would help as many homeless families as I could and help them find shelter, food and also clothing I would really like to accomplish as much as I can in life.

by Eli Eyre

Mom,

    I'm sorry for the way I acted today. I know that when I was doing my job I was kind of yelling at you! I know that was wrong and I'm very sorry. I guess it was because I'm sooo tired. I will try my very best to say "yes mommy," I promise. I want you to know that I love you very, very, very much, and I always will! You're the best mom in the whole entire world! I'm very sorry, *please* forgive me!

Love,

Shawnalee (your daughter) [11]

P.S. Give dad some hugs and kisses for me!

P.P.S. I'm sorry about the way I acted about going ice-skating today too! (please forgive me)

After a bad day at school, Charity at eight wrote:

Dear Mom,

    At school evryone was relly mean to me. For example Jordan makes me feel relly stupid in front of the whole clas evry second and Ms. Lisonbee made me cry. She was so rude. I dinnet know what to do when she told me I was being silly and to do somthing else so I just wrote to you.

Love You Lots,
Charity

From a study-abroad program in Jerusalem Saydi, nineteen, writes:

Dear Mom—

I can't believe I am here. It is all like a dream. It is too amazing. I feel like I should be watching myself in a movie. I am in the Holy Land. I still can not fathom the experience. I am so blessed Mom. Thank you so much for making this possible. Mom—I have been thinking a lot about you lately. I don't think I could ever express how much I love you. Mom you are absolutely incredible. I have learned so much from you. You have taught me how to have a sweet compassion for everything—for life in general. . . .

I have been thinking a lot. I don't think I have ever stretched this far into my brains. I have been thinking so much about how much I love you. Mom you are my mentor. I love you with all my heart. It is going to be so hard w/o you for so long. I rely so much on you. Your letters inspire me. Mom thanks for living such a great life and giving me so much. I love you!

Love,
Saydi

This was part of Eli's repentance process for going to a movie without telling us where he was—age eleven:

Dear Dad and Mom,

Why it is important to ask before going somewhere?

It is very important to ask before going somewhere so that people know where you are and people won't always be looking for you and they will know were you are and they won't be looking for you and be worried. It is also very important to ask because it is one of our family laws. When I forgot to ask last night it was very wrong because I broke one of the family laws and you guys were worried about me. I should have called very first thing and also asked before going to the movie. This would have made me feel a lot better and sure that you guys weren't worried. And it also would have made you guys sure that I was safe and not harmed. Asking is a very important thing to do, it makes everybody happy and not worried.

I should have probably even called during the movie, it would have made me a lot happier and not scared that you guys would be worried. I think that asking is a very important thing and I am very glad that we have it for a law because it will really help me to ask. I am really sorry for what I did. I feel really stupid. But I think writting this essay will remind me to call before going somewhere. This also teaches me not to break the family laws because there will always be a consequence if you break a law. I am really very sorry for not asking and I can assure you that this will never happen again. I am very sorry. I will always ask.

Love,
Eli Eyre

Sixteen-year-old Jonah writes:

Mom,

I love you! It is so simple but it compacts everything into three words. I love everything you do. Dad is a lucky guy you know it's going to take me my whole life to find a wife because you have set the standard. How do you do everything you do mil-lions of things a day to help people everywhere and some you don't even realize. Thank you for making food for me endlessly. I would be a shrimp if dad fed me (just kidding, not). You always seem to be able to make everything just perfect.

The words I love you can never be used enough and I could never make up all you have done for me in all my life but I'd better really get started. . . .

I love you,
Jonah

Roses are red,

vilites are blue,

I am glad I have a mom like you.

Some moms are funny

Some moms are kind,

some moms are totely

out of their mind.

But you mom—you're funny

you are pretty and kind

and you are sertenly not

out of your mind.

I LOVE YOU

and Happy Mother's Day

Love,

Saydi [12]

Found after coming home from a late meeting at midnight from thirteen-year-old Noah:

Mom,

After you left, the kitchen got more messed up so I figured that I had an opportunity to do what Jesus would do if he was here to help you. So I cleaned the kitchen, did the dishes, emptied dishwasher, and swept the floor on one condition, that condition is that *YOU GO TO SLEEP NOW!*

I love you and I'll see ya tomarow.

P.S. Have good dreams!

Dear Mom,

I like it wen you are happy. You are the best. I like it wen you say "my lips are chappy." I love you so much. I like your tuch. Thank for evrythig. You are a lovly thing.

Love,

Charity Eyre [7]

From Wellesley College came this letter from Saren, just as she was about to graduate.

Mom,

HAPPY BIRTHDAY.

I just want to tell you that you are about the most fabulous person on the face of the earth. I honestly don't know how to even express how *much* I appreciate you! My life has been so perfect in so many ways and I can only thank you for the support, the help, the confidence, the love you've always given me. Thanks for bringing me to college and helping me get settled in. I still miss you waking me up in the mornings and talking to me about the day. Thanks for all the sweet packages and the numberless postcards that made me feel so loved and involved when I felt so far away. Thanks for doing my hair in that special bun for Miss Christie's nativity scene when I was six and an angel. Thanks for that great birthday party when I turned five that I still remember. Thanks for the special dinners and for having Thanksgiving at our house instead of Zanavo. Thanks for teaching me violin and piano. Thanks for accompanying me so much. Thanks for being patient when I didn't want to practice. Thanks for coming to every performance. Thanks for telling me I'm smart and capable and making me that way. Thanks for suffering the hard times with me and for rejoicing in the good times with me. Thanks for goodness and light, sweetness and pride, past and future, and all that's good in life!

Love,
Saren [21]

Mom,

I love you so much I hope you have a great b.day. You're the greatest mom in the hole world.

I cry whenever I think of how great you are. I WOULD NOT BE

ABLE to live with out you I would Be flunking every class and Be
on the rong track I love you so much.

Love,
Talmadge Eyre [11]

P.S. You're the greatest

Dearest Mom,

Thanks for all you do for me. There are so many things, I
could not write them all down in a year, but I'll write a few.
Thanks for the meals you cook. (My favorite is Mashed Potatoes.) Thanks for your sugeschuns on playing violen or flute. I
think I'll take them. Take that back. I will take them. Also thank
you for your support in singing and dancing. Thank you for your
driving me to my classes, and helping me practice.

Love you lots,
Charity [8]

Thanks, I needed that (she screams and cries the entire time)—Mom.

Dear Mom,

You are the GREATEST! Thank you so much for all your help this
week. You are so cute to spend so much time learning the ac-
compianment (or however you spell it). You did just great. I
don't know, seriously how I would ever survive w/o you and
dad. You guys are simply the best.

I am really sorry for times when I get snotty and yell and have
a lot of crisises! I'll try and keep it under control!
I love you with/all my heart,

Saydria [17]

Dear Mom,

I love you. I missed you when you were gone.

When Grandma was here [Grandma J.], She said the only

thing wrong with me is that I wine to much. So, she made a deal with me it is that she will give me five dollars if I don't wine for on hole week. I am going to try it this week.

Will you remind me if I start to wine?

Thanks,

From Shawni [8]

P.S. Please don't tell anyone except dad.

(Since this was fifteen years ago, I figure it's okay to tell.)
Shawni, at twenty-two, from Romania:

Mom I love you more than I can *ever ever ever* express. In Isaiah it says "my people shall dwell in a peaceable habitation, and in sure dwellings, and in quiet resting places." I love it cause that is what our family is. It is such a sure dwelling and a quiet resting place—it is so pure and full of love and comfort. I feel *so* thankful for you and dad. You are so amazing, and you are my best friends. Sometimes I feel like our family is a little sauna of pure love or something and like I am out here in Antarctica or something, but then I get letters and it's *so* good. Oh, I love you *so* much.

Mom I miss you *so* much. You & Saren & Saydi are my best friends in the whole world (of *course* with the whole rest of the family), & I cannot wait to stay up and talk and talk about everything. I am *so* thankful to be a missionary. I am so thankful for guidance from Heavenly Father. I am *so* thankful for the gospel & that I have grown up with it in the best family in the entire world. I am *so* thankful for your never-ending support. I know how busy you are but you take out so much time for us. It means more to me than you will ever know. I love you with all my heart. It's frustrating cause I just can't tell you enough.

Love,

Shawni

Just after his arrival in England for two years of missionary service, Josh writes:

Dear Mom,

I'm sitting here eating Hobnobs, drinking Ribena and listening to Pachelbel . . . in LONDON. That's right. My first assignment on this 24 month labor of love is in the Catford area of London. This is going to be the hardest thing I've ever done, but there's no place on earth I'd rather be right now. I love the Lord so much, and I love serving him. I know I've have a lot to learn and I have a lot of room for improvement, but I know I can do it with the Lord's help. My soul delighteth in the scriptures!

London is a perfect place to start because there are so many people in a small area and about 80% are from countries other than England. I'm learning so much about other cultures. We are working with a wonderful family from Ghana. They are so bright and eager to learn. The food from Ghana is pretty interesting too . . . especially since the only utensils we use to eat it with is our hands.

The rain has finally stopped and now it is FREEZING. Our flat has no heating except for little portable heaters so when I go out of our room in the mornings, I take the heater with me and the rest of our flat is just as cold as it is outside.

Missions teach you so dang much—about turning the other cheek, about dealing with disappointments, about dealing with people (mean people, over-nice ones, and companions' annoying habits). It is a little microcosm of what life is all about.

Your letters mean so much to me. I read them over and over until I almost have them memorized. The longer I am away from home, the more I realize how blessed I am to have such a great family. Thanks for the package Mom. It made me happier than you can ever know!

Love up to the moon and back again.
Josh

My Christmas present from Saren at twenty-four when she was in Bulgaria:

Mom,

Merry Christmas!

I want to thank you with all my heart for giving me so many fond Christmas memories. Thank you for all the Christmas shopping you always did—searching to fulfill our silly wants. Thanks for the dolls and dresses and so many other thoughtful things. Thanks for so many Jerusalem Suppers and Christmas eggs benedict brunches. Thanks for children for Children Concerts and unending Ensemble rehearsals—sawing away at sorry Christmas carols. Thanks for staying up late and getting up early to make things just right for us. Thanks for letting me decorate and yielding to my insistance on having everything just so! Thanks for all the words of comfort and shared tears. I LOVE YOU!

Saren